Travel Her Way
~ Around the World

**An accommodation and holiday guide
for women travellers at home and abroad.**

Pat Bonner and Brenda Isles

2nd Edition

Pisces Publishers

Travel Her Way - Around the World 1997-1998
First published in 1997 by Pisces Publishers
17 Knotts Close,   Dunstable, Beds   LU6 3NY

Made and printed and bound in Great Britain
by Guernsey Press Co, Ltd., Guernsey, C.I.

ISBN 0 9525809 1 8

The authors and publishers would like to thank all persons involved
in providing information for the entries featured in this book who
have allowed us to use their details and their drawings.

Acknowledgements

We would like to thank all our readers for giving us details of what they needed in this second edition - your help was greatly appreciated.

We would also like to thank all our contributors for helping make 'staying away' a positive experience for our women travellers.

Last but not least, our thanks to Karen at Guernsey Press, who was so patient during two postponements for printing due to the ill-health of one of the authors.

Introduction

At last! The second edition of Travel Her Way! The new book has been a long time coming but we believe you will be delighted with the enormous increase in choice of accommodation, tours and holidays. In particular it should please those of you who asked us to research and include more places for women who preferred to travel and holiday abroad.

The task of compiling and producing the second edition has proved as time consuming as ever! We hope our efforts are visible through the variety of entries and information contained in these pages. We were determined to ensure that entries provided sufficient detail to help you make an informed choice - if only whether to send for a brochure!

Those involved in offering accommodation and holidays in this book are committed to supporting women travellers. We hope, that by making use of what's on offer, you will have the opportunity to meet like-minded women with whom you can share time and build friendships.

We do hope you enjoy and use the range of accommodation and holidays in this new edition and we welcome your comments about any of the entries - for better or worse! It's your comments that help us make decisions about entries in future editions.

May the providers and users of the accommodation, activity holidays, expeditions and courses enjoy a mutually rewarding experience. Your combined efforts in supporting one another make the production of this book worthwhile.

As always, happy travelling!

CONTENTS

England, Wales, Scotland and Ireland

CONTENTS

England, Wales, Scotland and Ireland continued

Page No.

CONTENTS

England, Wales, Scotland and Ireland continued

Page No.

CONTENTS

France, Belgium, Holland, Germany, Sweden

Page No.

CONTENTS
Spain, Italy, Malta

CONTENTS
India

CONTENTS

Canada and USA

Page No.

CONTENTS

Canada and USA continued

Page No.

CONTENTS

Australia and New Zealand

Terms used in Travel Her Way ~ Around the World

Women only   This describes an entry which accepts women only. Where children are accepted, this may include children of either gender, but acceptance usually carries an age restriction. Please check with individual owners.

Women/Woman run   This describes an entry where the owners/proprietors are women. The owners are certainly women friendly, but do not run a women only establishment.

Women friendly   This describes an entry where the owners are committed to supporting women travellers but the establishment is not women only. This description may include an entry where the owners/proprietors are a male and female couple.

England, Wales, Scotland
and Ireland

Helen and Kate's Women's B&B
Stoke Newington, Hackney
London N16
Tel: 0181 809 0891

Women only. Private home. Two double bedrooms. Shared bathroom. Tea/coffee making facilities. B&W TV in bedrooms. Garden. Table tennis. Exclusively vegetarian. Vegans catered for with notice. Children welcome. No pets. No smoking in house. Washing machine, iron, hairdryer available. Use of telephone on request (at cost). Rates: £12.00 - £15.00 per person per night. Open most of the year. Details available.

This 100 year old Victorian terraced house is situated in a small quiet street. It is close to Manor House Underground station on the Piccadilly line, which has a direct line to Heathrow Airport and easy connections to Gatwick Airport or Central London.

The bedrooms are comfortably furnished, with TV and refreshments. One room has French windows with views onto the garden, the other bedroom provides pleasant views of the street. The house has a basement where guests can play table tennis. Helen and Kate also have a piano which guests can request to use. The kitchen is not available to guests during the evening. However, their are very good eating and entertainment facilities locally, including two women's bars, a local jazz bar and a lively local park with an excellent café.

Helen and Kate are both active in women's lesbian and gay networks. Between them they speak German, French, Italian and Spanish. Helen and Kate have opened their home as a B&B for the last four years and have welcomed women from all over the world. They have full time jobs so do not serve breakfast, but leave everything ready for guests to prepare their own in the large, friendly kitchen which has doors leading into the garden.

Guests are provided with keys and an information folder giving details of London's transport and places to visit in London. More locally, Hackney enjoys a rich mix of cultures and has a large lesbian and gay community.

Reeves Hotel for Women
48 Shepherds Bush Green
London W12 8PJ
Tel/Fax; 0171 740 1158

Women only hotel. Five double and seven twin bedrooms. Eight bedrooms are en suite. Two shared bathrooms. TV. Hairdryer. Tea and coffee making facilities. Use of washing machine, iron and telephone on request. Licensed, with bar. Garden. Car park. Snacks available. Vegetarians and vegans catered for. No smoking during breakfast. Children welcome. £20+, per person per night. Discounts for longer stays. Open all year. Brochure available.

The Reeves Hotel is ideally situated for all of London's activities. It is only 10 minutes from Oxford Circus and there is easy access to Kew, Richmond and Heathrow airport.

Within walking distance of the West End, guests have an unlimited choice of things to do. There are interesting places to shop, ranging from the bustle of Oxford Street and the glitz of the Trocadero, to the bookshops in and around Charing Cross Road, like Silver moon, which specialises in women's literature. Worth a visit are the specialist food and cookery shops of Soho and the elegant stores along Regent Street and Piccadilly. There are many interesting galleries, art auction houses and museums in this area, plus, of course a wide choice of theatres and cinemas.

Kew Gardens, which covers Greenwich Park, has the largest children's playground of any Royal Park and also houses the Wilderness, with its area of wild flowers and woodland where deer graze. Greenwich Park is most famous for its Old Royal Observatory, the original home of Greenwich Mean Time, standing as it does on zero meridian longitude.

If you visit Richmond Park, you will get the opportunity to see herds of deer grazing in the heart of London.

55 Stanhope Road
Croydon, CRO 5NG
Tel: 0181 688 8882

Women only. Large house. One double room with en suite bathroom, three twin bedrooms and 2 single bedrooms. Three shared bathrooms. Tea and coffee making facilities. All rooms have colour TV and hairdryers. Visitors lounge with baby grand piano, colour TV and french windows to garden. Off street parking. No children. No pets. Open throughout the year. Bed and breakfast from £12.00 per person per night.

Built in 1903, as a rectory for St Matthews Church, this large unique Edwardian house, surrounded by landscaped water gardens, is tucked away in the beautiful Park Hill area of Croydon. All amenities are within easy walking distance. The Whitgift Shopping Centre and the infamous Fairfield Halls and Ashcroft Theatres are only 5 minutes walk.

East Croydon mainline station takes 20 minutes to London Victoria. Travellers can also connect to Gatwick Airport. For those wishing to drive, Gatwick is only 40 minutes from the house. There is access to the M25 and M23 road to Brighton. This is a good base from which to explore London or the South coast. Newcomers to Surrey may be surprised to find such attractive and deeply rural countryside so close to London.

Visitors may also want to consider trips to the Kent countryside, also within striking distance. It is excellent for walking and gives you the chance to see the many orchards, hop gardens, timber framed cottages and oast houses typical of the area.

At the house every first Saturday of the month is 'Dolly's'. This monthly event provides an exclusive meeting place for women, where they can enjoy good food, music and dancing and a raffle. Entry is by advance reservation only. Guests are requested to 'bring your own drink'. So - book a weekend away - Maureen will look forward to hearing from you.

Comment: The house is quite something and your host will make you very welcome.

21

Glory Mill Lane
Wooburn Green
Bucks HP10 0BX
Tel: 01628 522472

Women only. Private home. One-twin-bedded room. Shared bathroom. TV in bedroom. Log fire. Sitting room. Garden. Smoking allowed in the garden only. Dogs welcome if well-behaved. Washing machine, iron, telephone available. Dinner can be provided with advance notice. Open all year. Discounts for longer stays. Rates: £15.00 - £20.00 per person per night. Brochure available.

The house is part of a Victorian terrace in the village of Wooburn Green, situated in the middle of lovely countryside, near Marlow, Henley and Maidenhead. It has one twin-bedded room, with shared bathroom. Guests have access to the owner's sitting room, which is warmed by a log fire on cold evenings. The house has a small, pretty garden, at its best in the summer, for guests to enjoy.

The local area is rich in wildlife and one can even view ducks on a mill stream from the bedroom! Wooburn Green is ideally situated for a relaxing break or as a base for trips into London, which is less than an hour away to the east. The village has a glass works with craft demonstrations. There are some lovely walks passing through an interesting and varied area - including the Chiltern woodlands. There is an RSPB reserve at Hedgerley and the stately homes, Waddesdon House and Ascot House, are both open to the public. Benjamin Disraeli lived at Hughenden Manor and Florence Nightingale at Claydon House.

Visitors can head west to visit the famous town of Oxford. Ancient towns and villages, like Amersham and Chesham lie tucked away in the folds of the hills. To the south, the Thames meanders to within a few miles of Wooburn Green. Walk along the Thames towpath, explore the pretty village of Hambleden and enjoy the beauty spots of Boulters Lock and Bray, famous for punting. Visit Milton's cottage at Chalont St-Giles, also the Chiltern open-air museum, where ancient buildings have been re-erected.

Acacia House B&B
Loose
Near Maidstone, Kent
Tel: 01622 741943

Women only. Detached country house. Two double, one twin bedrooms. Shared bathroom. Tea and coffee making facilities, radio cassette and hairdryer. Use of iron on request. Garden. Barbecue. Off road parking. No smoking. No children or pets. Open all year. Rates from £20.00 per person per night. Brochure available.

Built of local ragstone in 1848 by local mill proprietor Joseph Amies, the house is set in a conservation area. To help you make the most of your stay there is an information folder in each bedroom which provides guests with details of activities round and about. One of the bedrooms overlooks the courtyard and the other two enjoy views of the garden, which is some two-thirds of an acre - so there's plenty of space in which to barbecue and relax privately.

Jackie has an interest in Spiritualism and Ann is Australian, with an interest in garden design. Their neighbours include four donkeys who really love polo mints!

Loose itself is very picturesque and has a stream running through the village. The area is excellent for walking and has easy access to public transport. The house is a good base from which to explore rural Kent, which boasts a number of castles, including Allington, Leeds, Hever and Rochester. Other sights include historic buildings, such as Boughton Monchelsea House, the friary at Aylesford, Churchill's home of Chartwell and Ightham Mote. Vita Sackville-West lived at Sissinghurst, only 20 minutes drive away and the gardens are open to the public. The local Kent scenery is really interesting and varied: hills, orchards, streams, the conical oast house of the hop gardens and picturesque half-timbered cottages. Maidstone offers shopping, cinema, theatres, ten pin bowling, a sports centre and a nightclub, plus the annual river festival.

Comment: You will be made very welcome by your hosts and the accommodation comes recommended. Definitely one to visit!

Bannings Guest House
14 Upper Rock Gardens
Kempton
Brighton, Sussex BN2 1QE
Tel: Geoff or Steve - 01273 681403

Women only. Three double, three twin bedrooms. Two of the bedrooms are en suite - all have showers. Colour TV. Radio alarm. Tea and coffee making facilities. Use of iron, hairdryer, telephone. Vegetarians, vegans and gluten-free diets catered for. The dining room and one of the bedrooms is non-smoking. No children. No pets. Closed December to February. Voucher parking outside house, free parking nearby. Discounts for longer stays. Rates: £17.00 - £21.00 per night. Brochure.

The house, which is part of a Georgian terrace, was built in 1807 for a maiden lady and her maid! It is now run by two men who enjoy catering and providing a safe environment for women. The house is tastefully decorated and has been awarded the 3 'Q's for quality by the Automobile Association. It is situated in a wide, leafy street leading down to the sea and is centrally located for all of Brighton's attractions. To ensure guests have maximum flexibility during their stay, a key will be provided for access.

Brighton can provide a host of things to do. The Lanes are a must, with a host of interesting shops, antique markets and restaurants. The town also has 3 museums, a leisure centre, 2 swimming pools, tennis and badminton courts, 4 cinemas and 6 theatres. There is a Natural Health Centre, a Women's Centre, Animal Sanctuary and Wildfowl Trust . This coast is ideal for windsurfing.

Inland, on the edge of the Sussex Downs is Lewes, a pleasantly unrushed country town. It has some attractive old buildings, mainly Georgian, but with a few older stone built or timber-framed specimens, particularly along its steep main street and in the little narrow alleys and other streets nearby. There are several good antique shops and an attractive complex of craft shops in a former candlemaker's factory in Market Lane.

Comment: Bannings has proved very popular with our readers and comes highly recommended.

Franklins
41 Regency Square
Brighton
Sussex BN1 2FJ
Tel: 01273 327016

Women run. Double, twin and single rooms available. All rooms en suite. TV. Room service. Dinner by prior arrangement. Snacks available. Fully licensed. Discounts for longer stays. Prices £24.00 - £28.00 per person per night. Further details available on request.

Franklins is a small, comfortable family run hotel. Sandra and Katrina, together with Sandra's two sister, pride themselves on providing a welcoming and relaxed atmosphere for all guests. The hotel is centrally situated close to all of Brighton's amenities.

All rooms have en suite facilities, central heating and colour TV. Room service is available from 11am to 11pm, offering a wide range of sandwiches and drinks, both alcoholic and non-alcoholic. Evening meals are available by prior arrangement.

Brighton stands out as a unique seaside town, with its own style and abundance of life. The combination of elegant Regency architecture, with Brighton's more shamelessly vulgar side, can be a lot of fun. For a rather more restrained atmosphere, visit Eastbourne, an interesting old fashioned seaside resort. Along the coast is Rye, a small town of great character.

The county of Sussex has a huge variety of scenery, including open downland, richly wooded valleys and hillsides, more sparsely wooded high heathland, prosperous farming country and a coast that runs from marsh, through sandy beaches, to chalk cliffs. It has some of England's most beautiful large gardens, some very attractive villages and small towns and a number of fine houses and castles.

Bed & Breakfast
Brighton, East Sussex
Tel: 01273 699720 or 674131

**Woman run B&B. One twin bedroom with shared bathroom.
Tea and coffee making facilities and hairdryer. Sitting room.
Washing machine, iron. Garden. Children welcome.
Babysitting by arrangement. Pets welcome. No smoking in
house. Snacks and packed lunches can be provided.
Vegetarians and vegans can be catered for with notice. Open
throughout the year. Rates: £8.00 - £12.00 per person per night
(sliding scale).**

You will receive a warm welcome to this restored Victorian terraced
house. It has a wood burning stove and there are attractive stripped
pine floors in the bedroom and lounge. It is very conveniently
situated for all the activities of Brighton and is within walking
distance of the town centre.

There are opportunities locally to experience the variety of
workshops and short courses on offer, eg 'drop-in yoga' and
complimentary therapy workshops.

Brighton is very welcoming to lesbians and gay men. It is culturally
and socially diverse. The sea is within walking distance and the
Downs, great for hikers, is a short bus ride away.

The Only Alternative Left
Women's Guest House
39 St Aubyn's
Hove, Sussex BN3 2TH
Tel: 01273 324739

**Women only. Guest house. Various room types. Tea and coffee
making facilities. Colour TV. Smoking area. Guest's
vegetarian kitchen for help-yourself breakfast. Garden. No
children. No pets. £10.00 - £15.00 per person per night.
Brochure available.**

The Only Alternative Left is a big house, just off the sea front and
about a mile from the centre of Brighton. The house an informal,
feminist atmosphere where all women can feel welcome and safe.
Every guest room has central heating and hot and cold water. There
is also a large sitting room with books, magazines, games and hi-fi,
which guests can enjoy. The main house is non-smoking but there
are ashtrays in the garden and a small smoking area is provided on
the ground floor.

The vegetarian kitchen is stocked with cereals, toast and preserves
for a help-yourself breakfast. It is also has a microwave and hot
plate if you want to make snacks. There are many late opening food
shops and restaurants nearby. Two that are recommended by the
hosts are 'Food for Friends' and 'Terre à Terre'.

Courses are sometimes run at the house and the group room, able to
seat up to 15, is available for hire. Details on request. Courses are
not necessarily women only.

Brighton is the most famous of the Sussex resorts with its Pier, the
Promenade and Pavillion. 'The Lanes' are maze of alleys small
squares, full of fascinating shops, a thriving antique trade and many
good pubs and eating places.

On Sunday mornings there is a good street market by the station
approach, but get there early to beat the antique dealers! Brighton
has a thriving gay community and an excellent number of gays pubs
and clubs to suit all tastes.

Hassocks, West Sussex
Tel: 01273 846524

Women only. House. One double bedroom. One single bedroom available at times. One shared bathroom. Tea and coffee making facilities and hairdryer. Sitting room. Washing machine, iron available. Sun room. Garden. No children. Well behaved neutered dogs accepted. Smoking in sun room or garden only. Dinner, snacks and packed lunches by arrangement. Special diets with notice. Open all year. Rates: B&B £10.00 per person, per night. Other meals extra.

The comfortable, informal detached house was built in the early 1900's. It is situated in a quiet residential road just a few minutes walk from the village, various shops, churches, a cafe and the mainline station. Hassocks is 8 miles north of Brighton.

The double bedroom is a large sunny, comfortable room at the front of the house. Your hosts will provide meals other than breakfast on request. They will try to cater for most special diets and welcome your input on any particular dietary requirements. Delicious home made jams and some home grown produce is available

There are several footpaths leading to the Downs if you wish to explore on foot, alternatively, the women have several different types of bicycle which they would be happy to lend guests. The two women share their home with two lovable dogs. Vanessa enjoys running and has run several half marathons. Marlene enjoys making and collecting teddy bears, as will be apparent to guests! They are a friendly, outgoing and non-conformist couple who enjoy meeting people and entertaining them. Their rates reflect the fact that they want to accommodate women who are willing to share their home on an informal basis.

A famous feature of the area is the pair of windmills, "Jack and Jill". They can be seen from the village, and are set on top of the Downs at Clayton. Devil's Dyke is a popular beauty spot with stunning views over Sussex and has a good pub and restaurant which is open all day, every day. There are many other places of interest including National Trust properties, Ditchling, Lewes and, of course, Brighton.

'A Woman's Place' in the New Forest
Tel: Molly - 01590 623310 or
Tel: Joyce - 01590 622184

Women only B&B guesthouse. Two double, one twin bedrooms. Lounge, TV room. Garden. Tea and coffee making facilities. Telephone, iron. Log fires. No smoking in house. Continental breakfast. All other meals available by prior arrangement. Vegetarian, vegan and gluten free diets catered for - please advise. Children accepted. Pets accepted. Open throughout the year. Rates: £17.50 per person, per night. Brochure available.

A Woman's Place is a cosy Edwardian country house, set in the heart of the conservation area of the New Forest. It is situated amongst woodland and heath, where ponies, cattle, donkeys, sheep and pigs roam free.

The guesthouse is conveniently situated within 10 minutes walk of a main line station and can be reached in 90 minutes from Waterloo. The market town of Lymington, with its marinas and ferries to the Isle of Wight, is a 10 minutes car or train journey away. Also within reach, by private or public transport, are Salisbury, Winchester, Bournemouth and Southampton, the latter two of which have a lively women's community.

Your hosts can provide vegetarian dinners for groups and even candlelit dinners with prior notice.

Your hosts already arrange walking weekends and healing weekends and they are currently planning other activity weekends - ask for details. They can provide information on how you can enjoy walking, cycling, sailing swimming and riding in the heart of the New Forest and Brockenhurst. If you want to see the New Forest by a less conventional method try going on a horse-drawn wagon ride, which will take you along routes where cars cannot go.

There are plenty of excellent places to eat and drink. There's also a wealth of places to visit - the New Forest owl Sanctuary, Lymington Vineyard, Breamore Houe and Museums, Lymore Valley Herb Garden and Lepe Country Park, to name but a few.

Jacqui Best
Keswick,
Wootton Grove, Sherborne
Dorset DT9 4DL
Tel: 01935 84369

Women only. One double and one single bedroom. Shared bathroom. Tea and coffee making facilities. TV and radio cassette player. Use of washing machine, iron, hairdryer and telephone on request. Sitting room/lounge. Garden. Smoking in garden and porch. Older children welcome. Pets accepted under certain conditions. Lunch, dinner, snacks and packed lunches available. Vegetarians catered for. Open throughout the year. Rates: £10.00 - £15.00 per person, per night.

The house is quiet and guests can enjoy the company of one another in the small comfortable lounge, which has a welcoming open fire. Guests can watch women's videos, listen to women's music and browse through books on women's issues.

Good vegetarian food is served and locally farmed organic food is used in food preparation wherever possible. Wine and beer is available with meals.

Jacqui collects books and articles on women's history and also speaks Italian. She can also offer therapeutic massage during your stay. Jacqui has a sound knowledge of the local area and can help you plan trips and provide you with details of any local women's events. Two mountain bikes are available for hire, or if you prefer to be on foot, Jacqui can point you in the direction of some excellent local walks. Maps are available.

Every second year Chard Women's Festival has top musicians and bands playing and is due to be held next in 1998. Chard is 30 minutes drive. The sea is about 40 minutes away by car. Also within walking distance is Sherborne, an attractive town with old world charm. The town is very pleasant to wander through and has tiny shops and tea rooms, a choice of book shop and markets and several fetes throughout the season. Sherborne Castle, built by Sir Walter Raleigh in 1594, is a fascinating, fully furnished historic house, with interesting paintings and porcelain and gardens.

The Studio
52 Broad Street
Lyme Regis DT7 3QF
Tel: 01297 442653/442616

Women only. Studio flat for holiday breaks. Two double bedrooms with en suite bathroom. One three bedded room with shared bathroom. Tea and coffee making facilities and TV in rooms. Lounge and large kitchen-cum-dining room. Garden. Continental breakfast. Special diets catered for with advance notice. No children (accommodation unsuitable). Pets welcome. No smoking in bedrooms. £12.50 per person per night for double occupancy with 2 nights minimum stay. Sorry, no single occupancy. Open most of the year. Let as a self-contained flat, suitable for up to 7 persons, during school summer holidays - Rates are £300 per week Saturday to Saturday. Please note: steep stairs.

The Studio forms part of a complex, together with the Antique Shop and Old Bakehouse at the bottom of the garden and is run by Katie and Susie who will be remembered for providing holiday accommodation for women at Eagle House for over 15 years.

Lyme Regis is a lovely old-fashioned seaside resort known as "The Pearl of Dorset" and was the location of the film The French Lieutenant's Woman by local author John Fowles.

There are stunning coastal walks and an abundance of nature trails. The area has a profusion of fossils, including dinosaur bones, found along its beaches. During the season there are many regular events, including a jazz festival, lifeboat and carnival weeks. The local cinema shows early-release films and the theatre has excellent productions. There are also interesting shops and galleries. Dorchester, Taunton and Exeter are all about 27 miles away. For those without their own transport, the area can be reached in 2½ hours by train from Waterloo, or there is a National Express coach service.

Inland is a rich mixture of downland, lonely heaths, fertile valleys, historic houses and lovely villages of thatch and mellow stone buildings.

Sheila Gwyn
Wild Rose Women's Holidays
S.E. Cornwall
Tel: 01752 822609

Women only. Holiday house for women - up to 8 residential places. Two bathrooms. Two sitting rooms. Linen and duvets provided. Please bring own towels. Food is vegetarian. No smoking indoors. No pets. Price is all inclusive of chosen activity, breakfast, packed lunch and evening meal. Typical price for a 4 night walking holiday is £139.00 p/p. Brochure.

This holiday house has evolved over the past few years to become an attractive, peaceful retreat where women can come together to have interesting, inspiring and relaxing holidays. Holidays are on specific dates and are based on a special interest, such as walking, writing, singing, drumming etc. Some holidays, such as Pot Luck, Easter Special, Christmas and New Year, are varied and include different activities. All are particularly suitable for women holidaying alone and there is free transport from the station.

Sheila, who runs Wild Rose, leads the walking holidays which can be either gentle or energetic. Nothing is compulsory and guests are free to take time out to do their own thing at any time. Sheila's vegetarian home-cooking is delicious and nutritious. There are plenty of fresh vegetables, salads, fruits and delectable desserts. Everyone eats together around an old pine table and guests are free to make hot drinks whenever they wish.

The house is situated in beautiful, rolling countryside close to superb sandy beaches. The peninsula is peaceful and undeveloped, with many different vistas of coast, rivers, estuaries and wooded valleys. The house itself is full of plants and flowers and has a large selection of books and maps which guests may borrow. Welcoming log fires blaze whenever it is chilly outside. The garden is secluded and there are patio areas for basking in the sun.

From 1996 Sheila has been running women's holidays in other venues, notably on the Lizard, SW Cornwall based at a National Trust Hotel (7 days for £159.00) and on the Mediterranean island of Gozo, Malta (7 days half-board in a 4 star hotel is £239.00).

Penryn House Hotel
The Coombes
Polperro
Cornwall PL13 2RG
Tel: 01503 272157

> **Woman run hotel. Various types of room, from standard single to superior en suite. Tea and coffee making facilities. TV. Licensed bar. Restaurant. Dinner, lunches, packed lunches and bar meals available. Vegetarians catered for. Sun Terrace. Children welcome. Dogs by prior arrangement. Parking. Attractive mid-week rates available November to mid-March. Rates from £20.00 per person per night with reductions for longer stays. Brochure available.**

Penryn House Hotel is located on the main village road into Polperro and has been awarded 3 crowns by the English Tourist Board. You will be among the few visitors allowed to drive into the village as there is a spacious car park for guests. The hotel has a tranquil setting where you will be looked after. Relax in the well-stocked fireside lounge bar or enjoy imaginative food in the restaurant which makes use of local produce and fresh sea food.

Lunches can be taken in the bar or on the sun terrace. Packed lunches are also available on request. Dogs are accepted by prior arrangement at a small charge per night. Regrettably, dogs are not allowed in the communal rooms.

Various activity breaks specifically for women only are organised throughout the year. These include Pub Walks, Golf Breaks, Strictly Singles, New Year Celebrations, St Valentines and Thanksgiving.

Polperro village is renowned for its quaint, narrow lanes and whitewashed cottages. It still retains its old world charm. Step back a few centuries to explore the past and splendour of the Cornish heritage and take life at a more leisurely pace. Visitors can shop, eat out, walk the coastal paths with their breathtaking vistas, or just relax amongst friends at the hotel.

'Capistrano'
1 Chy-An-Dour Square
Penzance
Cornwall TR18 3LW
Tel: Sylvia 01736 64189

Women run. Cottage. One double bedroom with washbasin. Shared bathroom. Tea and coffee making facilities. TV. Garden/patio. No children. No pets. Use of hairdryer and iron on request. Vegetarians catered for. Car parking. Open March - October. Prices seasonal from £14.00 - £16.00 per person per night.

This is a 100 year old granite cottage, with private walled garden and patio. It is located on the outskirts of Penzance in a quiet cul-de-sac. The guest double bedroom enjoys sea views. The upstairs toilet is adjacent to this bedroom and there is also a shower room and further toilet downstairs. There is on street parking outside the cottage.

Penzance has a large selection of interesting shops, good eating places and pubs. The byways and curio shops, as well as the sub-tropical gardens, are well worth exploring on foot. Penzance has a busy harbour from which visitors can take fishing trips. Also available are day trips to the Scilly Isles by boat or helicopter. Penzance has both an open-air swimming pool and sea water pool.

Nearby are many places of interest, cliff path walks, pre-historic sites, standing stones, iron age forts and, of course, Lands End. Much of the land is uncultivated, unfenced ancient heathland. The castle and tiny fishing village on the little eyelet of St Michael's Mount can be visited on foot at low tide, or by boat at high water. The area's strongest appeal is to people who love the outdoors and who enjoy feeling the wind in their hair. In Winter it is milder than most places, with violets out along the cliffs, even in January.

Ask Sylvia for details of what's on during your visit. There is a bus and train station within 10 minutes walk of the cottage and access by rail and road is good.

Goldsithney Gallery
York House, Fore Street, Goldsithney
Penzance, Cornwall TR20 9LG
Tel; 01736 711129

**Women only. House. One twin bedroom. Private shower
bathroom with sink and WC. Tea and coffee making facilities.
TV. Iron. Garden. No children. No pets. Smoking permitted.
Packed lunches available on request. Vegetarian and vegan
diets catered for by prior arrangement. Open throughout the
year. Rates: £15.00 p/p per night, all year round. Brochure.**

York House is Georgian and built of granite with beamed ceilings.
The front of the house has, for many years, served as a shop and is
now run by the owners as a gallery and studio, where the work of
local artists is displayed, including prints, paintings, ceramics and
jewellery.

The bedroom has two twin beds that can combine to create a double
bed. The room is light and sunny and has double aspect windows
and a breakfast table where guests have views of the village.

The garden is large and attractive, with palm trees and bay trees and
guests are welcome to take home a supply of fresh bay leaves.
There are also apple trees and a fish pond. Why not have breakfast
in the garden? When the weather is good it makes a lovely spot to
sit, eat breakfast and plan your activities for the rest of the day.

Breakfast sounds delicious and is very ample, with a choice of cold
or cooked food, including a vegetarian or vegan choice available if
required. To complete the service, the two women are planning to
keep a few chickens so that guests can enjoy fresh eggs!

Ingrid is an artist who specialises in etchings. She works in her
studio which is a converted barn at the back of the house. Her work
is displayed in the gallery. Jean is a journalist, writer of fiction and
drama and a photographer.

To inform anyone who has an allergy to fur or fear of dogs, the
house as a resident Irish Setter. For those who enjoy dogs, she has a
wonderful temperament and most guests want to take her home!

The Old General Store - Antiques and Curiosities
Fore Street, Goldsithney
Penzance, Cornwall TR20 9HD
Tel: Joan or Valerie on 01736 711 711

Women only B&B apartment. One double bedroom with en suite. Additional single bed available in sitting room if required. Bedroom has tea and coffee making facilities, Colour TV, ironing board and iron, hairdryer, board games, book and fridge. Sitting room. Candlelit dinners.   Children welcome. Babysitting service and children's menu. Pets welcome. Smoking permitted. Lunch, dinner, snacks and packed lunches available. Most special diets catered for with notice. Open throughout the year. Rates: £16.50 per person per night for double occupancy. Single occupancy is £20 per night.

Situated in a village location, the flat is above the owners' Antiques shop and has its own front door. The accommodation is one mile from the sea and St Michael's Mount, 4 miles from Penzance and 7 miles from St Ives.

Your hosts have considerable experience in the hospitality business and are able to offer quality accommodation and gourmet cooking. Home grown produce is used in food preparation and food is good and plentiful.

There is plenty for guests to do locally. Penzance has many interesting shops, good eating places and pubs. The curio shops, byways and tropical gardens are well worth exploring on foot. Penzance has an open-air swimming pool and a sea water pool.

Goldsithney is an ideal base for visits to St Ives, Mousehole, Lands End, Prussia Cove, The Lizard and Zennor, none of which are more than 30 miles distant. There are many lovely walks from and around Goldsithney. The village has 2 pubs, both serving excellent meals, a grocery store, post office. The village also has a regular bus service into Penzance. The nearest beach is Perranuthno, which is 5 minutes drive or 20 minutes walk and it has a coastal path in either direction.

Near to Woolacombe
North Devon
Tel: 01271 870497

Women only. Self-catering converted barn. One double bedroom/lounge plus kitchen/dining room. TV and radio/cassette. Fridge, washing machine, hob oven and iron. Cloakroom and shower. Pets welcome. Open throughout the year. Prices seasonal from £100.00 - £150.00 per week. Winter breaks available. Brochure available.

This converted stone barn is attached to a 17th century thatched cottage but has its own separate entrance and parking space. Visitors can enjoy complete privacy in over an acre of secluded gardens. Loungers are provided. Views extend across open farmland to Exmoor and Dartmoor.

Guests' privacy is respected, although the owners are also happy and willing to help visitors make the most of their visit by sharing their knowledge of the surrounding area. Your hosts enjoy walking the two Moors, windsurfing, gardening (specialising in herbs), painting and reading.

There are exceptional coastal walks within half a mile. Sandy Woolacombe beach is less than a mile distant and can be reached via the fields at the back of the garden (about 25 minutes walk). There are also good beaches at Saunton and Croyde. All three beaches have gently sloping shorelines for safe swimming. For the more adventurous, there is usually good surf if you go out into deeper waters. Braunton Burrows is a nature reserve for orchids, other wild flowers and birds. The sand dunes extend over many miles to Crow point, where you can sail and windsurf in relative safety. Braunton, 4 miles away, is the largest village in Britain, with the best fish and chip shop in the area and an excellent gallery of crafts and paintings.

There are many art galleries at Lynton, Lynmouth and Porlock, where local artists of some standing exhibit work which captures the beauty of the coast and the moors. Good restaurants and pubs, offering a wide variety of food, can be found in abundance- usually at very reasonable prices.

Hillview Guest Houe
Woodlands
Combe Martin
Devon EX34 0AT
Tel: Jackie 01271 882331

Women run guest house. Four double, one twin bedrooms, of which 2 are en suite. TV and Tea and coffee making facilities in all rooms. Hairdryer, iron, telephone and clothes drying facities and packed lunches available on request. Vegetarians catered for. No smoking. No pets. Prices seasonal £14.00 - £16.50 per person per night. Closed November-March (Open Easter). Brochure available.

Hillview, situated at the end of a private drive, is in a quiet sheltered position, but still within easy walking distance (500 yards) of sea and local village pubs. It is one of five, large Edwardian houses built by a local land owner (one for each of his children). Guests have access to the sitting room and garden. There is a sheltered verandah on which to sit and dream and watch the sun set! From the house there are views of grazed hills, studded with mature oaks and beech, where buzzards nest.

Jackie is a keen walker and birdwatcher, therefore lots of pathfinder maps and guide books are available. Guests can also hire cycles locally to explore the famous 'Tarka the Otter' trail.

The south west coastal path follows along the cliff tops on to Combe Martin, once the centre of a thriving silver mining industry. The National Trust and Exmoor National Park organise guided walks including walks to see herds of red deer and Exmoor ponies. Eight miles to the west are wide sandy beaches ideal for surfing and swimming (Woolacombe, Croyde and Saunton Sands). Lundy Island is a marine nature reserve and can be reached by boat from Ilfracombe or Bideford. The National Trust house of Arlington Court, once the home of Ms Chichester (great aunt of Sir Francis) and her companion, is well worth a visit.

Helen and John Christian
'Woodlands'
Lynbridge, Lynton
North Devon EX35 6AX
Tel: 01598 752324

Women friendly hotel. 4 double, 2 twin and 2 single bedrooms. 5 bedrooms are en suite. Tea and coffee making facilities. TV and radio in all rooms. Lounge. Log fire. Garden. Drying room. Car Park. Licensed bar. No smoking in house. Evening meal with vegetarian choice. Packed lunches. Children over the age of 12 years. No pets. Washing machine, tumble dryer, iron, telephone, available. £16.00 - £22.00 per person, per night. Discounts for longer stays. Open March to October inclusive. Brochure available.

Helen and John welcome women travelling alone, together and as couples (partners). They took over the hotel in August 1994 after travelling for two years in India and South East Asia. Helen tends to be the 'front of house' person and has more contact with guests. John is an excellent cook and enjoys being creative in the kitchen.

Woodlands is in a peaceful location, situated on high ground overlooking Summerhouse Hill and the unspoiled wooded valley of the West Lyn river. Five of the bedrooms are particularly spacious, with lovely views of the valley opposite the hotel. One bedroom has a balcony. Guests can relax in front of the log fire in the cosy sitting room in the cooler months. Food is home cooked, using the best of local produce. The 3-course evening meal includes a vegetarian choice. Guests are welcome to use the hotel's garden.

Lynton and Lynmouth are friendly villages with tea rooms, restaurants, pubs, churches, shops and a museum. Woodlands is ideally situated on the edge of both villages and is an excellent place to stay when exploring North Devon and beyond. Exmoor has 680 miles of footpaths and bridleways, offering superb coastal and moorland walks, many of which are accessible by foot from the hotel.

Comment: This hotel has proved very popular with our readers. The welcome is warm and friendly and the food is excellent.

Somerset Levels
Near Langport
Tel: Mel on 01458 253401

> **Women only cottage. One double bedroom. Shared bathroom. TV and video, tea and coffee making facilities. Bedroom has sofa and seating area. Garden. Telephone and iron. No children. Pets accepted. Careful smokers only (thatched cottage!). Open throughout the year. Rates: £15.00 per person, per night. Whole space available on request. Brochure available.**

This very attractive thatched cottage is the middle of three, set in rural countryside. It is a Grade II listed building constructed of local stone and retains its original beams.

The bedroom is beautiful - large and very welcoming, with plants and flowers and a beamed ceiling. It has a "huge" bed and from the windows guests can enjoy lovely scenic views.

You will be made welcome by your host and guests will find the atmosphere peaceful and relaxing. There is plenty of wildlife to observe as well as an ancient woodland behind the house. Mel has an interest in flower and crystal remedies, has local artwork for sale at the cottage, including cards and posters and can provide organic fruit and vegetables in season.

The delicious vegetarian breakfast includes home baked bread, eggs and fruits in season.

Local attractions include Glastonbury Abbey and Tor, Wells Cathedral, Mendips, Cheddar Gorge, Taunton, beautiful walking countryside, ancient hills and woodlands and the Somerset Levels.

Comment: We have had positive feedback from visitors who have recommended this "gorgeous" cottage. Mel is "lovely" and the home grown vegetables and freshly baked bread are delicious. For those who like board games, it seems Mel's good at Scrabble!

Deirdre Nash
21 Oxenpill
Meare, Near Glastonbury
Somerset BA6 9TQ
Tel: 01458 860719

Woman run. Self catering cottage sleeping 4 people in one double and one twin bedroom. Children welcome. Well behaved pets welcome (£5.00 per dog per week). Private bathroom. Colour TV. Garden. Rates: £120.00 - £270.00 per week, including electricity. Short lets and mid week breaks can be arranged out of season. Linen and towels can be supplied at £5.00 per person. Open all year. Brochure available.

April Cottage is situated in the tiny rural village of Westhay on the Somerset Levels. Dating from the 17th Century, this delightful stone-built cottage has retained many of its original features. Tastefully decorated, equipped and furnished to a high standard, it provides a comfortable holiday home from which to explore the lovely surroundings.

The large sitting room has a beamed ceiling, flagstone floor, beamed inglenook with exposed bread oven and open fireplace for log fires. The kitchen/diner has pine furniture and fittings, electric cooker, fridge-freezer and washing machine. Two pretty bedrooms are well furnished and have sloping ceilings, exposed stone walls and beams. A cot is available. The private sunny garden has been professionally designed and includes garden furniture and a brick built barbecue. The cottage is heated throughout by night storage heaters.

The Somerset Levels are a little known wilderness area ideal for walking, cycling and bird watching. There are many nature reserves nearby. Glastonbury Abbey and Tor, Wells Cathedral, Cheddar Gorge, the Mendip and Quantock Hills, Burnham with 7 miles of sandy beaches, are all within easy reach.

Women Only Bed and Breakfast
Bristol
Tel: 0117 977 2649

**Women only. Private house. On double, one twin and two
single bedrooms. Shared bathroom. Tea and coffee making
facilities. Lounge. TV room. No smoking in house. No pets.
Dinner available. Vegetarians and vegans can be catered for.
Open throughout the year. Rates from £14.00 per person per
night.**

This private house is situated in a quiet suburb of Bristol. It has
good bus links to the city centre and university and is an ideal base
for work, study or sight seeing trips. The owner has a keen interest
in local history and country walking and is happy to lead walks or to
lend books and maps to assist the independent walker.

The M5 runs the length of the county (Avon) and rail services are
fast and direct - Bristol to London takes approximately 1 hour.

Bristol has much to offer the tourist. The city's involvement in the
colonisation of the New World and the trade in sugar, tobacco and
slaves that followed, made it the second city in the kingdom in the
18th Century. On the old docks is the Bristol Industrial Museum
and the SS Great Britain, Brunel's famous 'iron ship'.

For a glimpse of Bristol's elegant past, stroll through Clifton with
its stately terraces and King Street, with its merchant seamens' alms
houses. King Street also contains the Theatre Royal - the oldest
theatre in continuous use in England.

Glastonbury, with its famous Tor and sacred healing well is just 1
hour away by bus. Try making the magnificent journey over the
Mendips via Wells Cathedral part of your itinerary.

Whilst in the area it is certainly worth making a visit to Bath, one of
the most loved historic cities in England. Bath owes its existence to
the hot springs which bubble up 500,000 gallons of water a day.

Strathmore
West Malvern Road
Upper Wyche,
Malvern, Worcs WR14 4EL
Tel: 01684 562245

Women only. Guest house. Two double bedrooms, Shared guest bathroom. TV. Electric blanket. Washbasin in bedrooms. Tea and coffee making facilities. Smoking in the Conservatory or Garden. Full English or Continental breakfast. Vegetarians catered for with advance notice. Garden. No children. No pets. Telephone and iron available. Discounts for longer stays. Open throughout the year. £16.00 - £20.00 p/p per night. Brochure.

Strathmore is a large, Victorian house standing in a ¼ acre of garden. It is built of locally quarried Malvern stone and is situated on the beacon. Rooms are available to guests all day. A separate bathroom with bath, shower, toilet and bidet is close to the bedrooms. A clothes drying facility is available. Guests can be sure of complete privacy, amidst tranquil surroundings and are welcome to use the garden and conservatory. Use of sitting room is available for larger parties. Breakfast is served in the first floor lounge.

The house has a magnificent panoramic view across Herefordshire. On clear days the Black Mountains, Hay Bluff, the Sugar Loaf at Abergavenny and the Brecon Beacons can be seen on the horizon. Sunsets are spectacular, especially in Autumn and Winter.

The Malvern hills, an area of outstanding natural beauty, have many walks and magnificent views. Herefordshire is renowned for its black and white houses. Ledbury has its famous Church Lane, often seen in the period TV films. The Malvern Festival takes place annually and the Three Counties Showground is in Malven Wells, where national events are staged throughout the year. There are railway stations at Malvern Link and Great Malvern and guests can be met at either station by prior arrangement.

Comment: Do take plenty of bottles to stock up with Malvern water at the local spring (10 minutes from the house). The host is very welcoming and the breakfasts are delicious. Lovely, very private garden with lots of nooks and crannies.

Oulton Broad
Near Lowestoft
Suffolk
Tel: 01502 515460

Women only. One bedroom with en suite bathroom. TV and radio. Tea and coffee making facilities. Sitting room and lounge. Hairdryer. Garden. No smoking in house. Vegetarians and other special diets catered for. Packed lunches and dinner available. No children. No pets. Off road parking. Rates £15.00 per person per night. Brochure available.

The two owners are happy to share their home with you and you can be sure of a friendly and warm welcome in a relaxed environment. They have extensive knowledge of the local area and can help you with your holiday plans. To assist guests, the owners are happy to provide free transport to and from the local railway and bus station. Collection from greater distances can be arranged for a small fee.

Accommodation is in the loft conversion of the bungalow, with an en suite shower and toilet. Guests can either join the owners in the communal areas of the house and indulge in interesting conversation and a G&T, or relax in their room. There is no extra charge for single occupancy.

The garden is also available for guests to enjoy. The owners are both keen gardeners and this is reflected in the abundance of plants, fruit trees and vegetables. Much of the home grown produce is used in the preparation of wonderful dishes - it's well worth staying for dinner!

Oulton Broad is an ideal centre for exploring the Norfolk and Suffolk coasts, and the Broads. It is also an excellent base for canoeing and water sports, cycling, walking and bird watching. There are also many musical events locally, including the Aldburgh festival. Minsmere (RSPB), Southwold, Walberswick, Snape and Norwich are within easy reach.

Comment: Loads of positive feedback on this entry! Start as guests and end as friends - even if you're only staying overnight! Try to stay for dinner - the food is very good!

The Old Exchange
45 Freeman Street
Wells-next-the-Sea
Norfolk NR23 1BQ
Tel: 01328 711362

Woman run. One double, one twin, one single bedroom. Two shared bath/shower rooms. Tea and coffee making facilities. TV and hairdryer in bedrooms. Iron and telephone available. No smoking. Vegetarians and vegans catered for. Private car park. Children welcome. Pets welcome. £16.00 - £20.00 per person, per night. Open throughout the year. Also caravan for hire from £60.00 to £200.00 per week.

The Old Exchange, originally an Inn, is over 200 years old. It has exposed beams and brickwork with a 16th century wall enclosing the garden. It is situated approximately 200 yards from the Quay.

The north Norfolk coast, a shoreline of long sandy beaches, is now officially protected for its beauty and wildlife. This area is one of the best places in England for birdwatchers all year round. The north of the county has a character all of its own and appeals to people who want to get away from it all. Wells-next-the-Sea has good local restaurants, serving fresh seafood in season.

Your proprietor, Jean, offers the use of her beach hut for changing and making cups of tea. There are stables nearby for horseriding on the beach. The hinterland has pine woods and the salt marshes are another haven for birdwatchers.

Jean runs a small second-hand books and bric-a-brac shop at The Old Exchange and, if you want to clear out your bookshelves or attic, she's happy to make you an offer.

Jean also has a caravan for hire on the Pinewoods caravan site, close to the beach. It has a double bedroom and a bunk-bedded room, TV, oven, fridge, radio and, of course, lots of books. Further details and availability on request.

Comment: Readers have said how welcoming Jean has been and how they have enjoyed their stay. People go back again!

Christine Parker and Simon Batty
Fieldview, West Barsham Road
East Barsham, Nr Fakenham
Norfolk NR21 0AR
Tel: 01328 820083
E-mail: 106100.362@compuserve.com

Women friendly guest house. Four double and five twin bedrooms. One bedroom is en suite. Four shared bathrooms and 2 shower rooms. Tea and coffee making facilities, TV and hairdryer. Lounge with TV. Garden. Log fires. Dinner, lunch, snacks and packed lunches are available. Special diets catered for. Two ground floor bedrooms and one ground floor bathroom with shower could be used by some disabled travellers. Access to breakfast room by 3 steps. No children. No pets. Open all the year. Rates: £20.00 per person per night. Brochure.

Situated in a rural area, near Fakenham, this modern house, built in a traditional manner can accommodate 18 people comfortably. It also has facilities for meetings and small conferences. Your hosts offer a particularly warm welcome to women travellers.

The house has a well placed garden, backing onto fields and parking space for 9 cars. There are scenic views from the bedrooms and the en suite Astronomer Royal bedroom also has velux windows, giving a fantastic view of the sky.

Fieldview is a new site for amateur astronomers and situated in an area of East Anglia that has a greater number of clear nights than average. Your hosts specialise in astronomy and run short courses for beginners. Fieldview has three reflecting telescopes. Guests are welcome to use the equipment and training is willingly given.

For non-astronomers, there are plenty of alternative activities and places of interest. The North Norfolk coast is designated an area of outstanding natural beauty. The wide sandy beaches alternate with high stately cliffs, offering delightful walks and superb landscapes. The many nature reserves and The Broads shelter a wide variety of birds and wildlife, making the area a gem for ramblers, cyclists, naturalists and birdwatchers. The stately homes, with their wonderful gardens are a must.

The Old Station House
4 Chatsworth Road
Rowsley, Near Matlock
Derbyshire DE4 2EJ
Tel: 01629 732987

**Women run. Three bedrooms, each with double and single beds.
One shared bathroom and one shower room. Tea and coffee
making facilities. Hand basin in rooms. Radio. Use of
hairdryer, iron and telephone on request. Sitting room/lounge.
TV room. Dinner and packed lunches available. Vegetarians
and vegans catered for. Children welcome. Pets welcome. No
smoking in bedrooms. Car park. Open all year. £14.00 -
£17.00 p/p, per night. Children £6.00- £9.00 per child per night.**

The Old Station House was built around 1850 and is thought to
have been the original Station Master's House for Rowsley Railway
Station. Now awarded 1 Crown (Commended) by the East
Midlands Tourist Board , this small, friendly establishment offers
traditional continental or vegetarian breakfasts. Evening meals are
available, using home grown produce in season and includes a 3-
course vegetarian option.

The house is situated at Rowsley, a moorland walking centre, on the
edge of the Peak National Park and all around are the hills and
lovely valleys of the Peak District. Visitors can walk to the local
stone circles, cycle, ride and fish. Cauldwell's Mill in Rowsley is
Europe's only working water-powered roller flour mill. It also
houses a fine craft centre, several craft workshops and a tea parlour.

Well situated for many famous Derbyshire attractions, the market
towns of Bakewell, Chesterfield and Ashbourne are within easy
distance. Also close to Rowsley is Haddon Hall and Chatsworth
House. Worth a visit is Matlock and its famous attractions and craft
workshops. There is a wildlife park at Riber Castle. Buxton, over
1000 feet up in the hills, is a spa that was laid out in the 18th century
to rival Bath. You can drink the waters which rise up from the hot
underground springs, attend the opera, or walk in the fine gardens
and shopping streets. Nearby is Eyam, the historic 'Plague Village'.
*Comments: Very hospitable. Breakfast was wonderful. Very clean.
Front bedroom can be noisy. We're going again.*

New House Farm Women's B&B
Near Hebden Bridge
West Yorkshire
Tel: 01422 885284

**Women only. Farmhouse. One family and one double bedroom.
Shared bathroom. Washbasin in each room. Use of hairdryer,
iron and telephone on request. Tea, coffee and fruit available.
Guest sitting room/lounge with TV and hi fi. Garden. Dining
room. Lunch, dinner, light suppers, snacks and packed lunches
available. Special diets catered for. Children welcome.
Children's menu. Babysitting available. No pets. Log fire. No
smoking. Closed Christmas Eve to Boxing Day inclusive. £17.00
per person per night maximum. Discounts for longer stays.
Brochure available.**

This is a grade II listed building which was a former farmhouse
with a barn attached, built in local stone. Situated in Midgley, a
small hilltop village close to beautiful heather moorland. The
accommodation is comfortable and fresh towels and toiletries are
provided for each guest. There is a bath/shower solely for guests'
use. Coal/log fires and candlelit dinners add to the feeling of
warmth, welcome and comfort.

Your hosts have their own free range eggs and vegetables in season.
Food is wholesome and plentiful. For walkers and those wanting to
explore, guests are welcome to use the variety of maps and guides to
the area. A selection of games, toys and books are available.

Footpaths to the Calderdale Way start from the house and there is
easy access to moorland walks. Hebden Bridge, an engaging small
town, is close by. It has a variety of specialist gift shops, an
excellent bookshop and lots of tea shops and antique shops. In
summer there are horse-drawn barge boats from the canal basin.
Close by is Hardcastle Crags, a National Trust woodland property
offering excellent walks. Just further afield is Haworth, where the
Brontës lived and, still within easy travelling distance are the Dales.

*Comment: Feedback has been very good. A warm, friendly
welcome, comfortable surroundings and lots of delicious food.*

The Amalfi Licensed Hotel
19-21 Eaves Street
Blackpool, FY1 2NH
Tel: 01253 22971

Women run hotel. Double and single rooms available. Full central heating. Own keys and access at all times. Tea and coffee making facilities. Colour TV Lounge. Fully licensed. Bar snacks available. Pets welcome. Open all year. Rates: £12.00 - £18.00 per person, per night for B&B in double or twin room. There is a single supplement. Special offer: Monday - Friday morning B&B at £45.00 per person. Brochure available.

Marlene and Helen welcome you to their hotel, which is only 1 minute from the sea front and 5 minutes from the various pubs and clubs, including Lucy's, Basil's, 501 and the Flamingo Club. The Amalfi is the only hotel in Blackpool owned and run by gay women for gay women and their families. The clientele is 95% gay women, with the remainder being mixed friends and family members.

Few towns in the country can provoke such a strong reaction as Blackpool. Love it or loathe it, it's impossible to remain unaffected by it. It has an infection and boisterous atmosphere. Most children will love it and, for those adults who are children at heart, this is the place to visit

Blackpool Tower concentrates on larger exhibitions and, where most towns have one pier, Blackpool has three. Blackpool Pleasure Beach is a huge entertainment area, with 150 spectacular and breathtaking rides, giving visitors an experience they'll never forget. In the Autumn the famous illuminations light up the Golden Mile and are probably the best of their kind.

There is plenty to do and see. Try a visit to Coronation Rock Co, where the famous Blackpool Rock is made. The Grundy Art Gallery houses a permanent collection of work by its 19th and 20th century artists. Blackpool Zoo is set in spaciously landscaped gardens with a miniature railway and play area.

Women's Holiday Centre Ltd
Horton-in-Ribblesdale
Settle, N. Yorks, BD24 0HD
Tel: 01729 860207

Women only and girls full board accommodation (and boys up to 10 years). Two double and two large family bedrooms. Two shared bathrooms. Sitting room. Open fires. Garden. TV room. Kitchen. Playroom. Use of washing machine, iron, hairdryer and pay telephone. Smoking downstairs only. The house is meat free. Vegetarians and vegans catered for. Disabled travellers welcome. Support dogs/guide dogs welcome. Courses and workshops. Car parking. Open all year. Rates: Sliding scale according to income. Camping facilities. Brochure

This is a unique organisation, set up in 1980, as a charity run by a women's co-operative to provide holidays for women on moderate or limited means, and their children. It survives mainly by donations, which can be made tax-free under the centre's charitable status. It is a safe and friendly environment where women can feel at home and get to know each other. There are two full time female workers at the centre.

The Centre is situated in the Old Vicarage in the village, at the foot of Pen-y-Ghent. Accommodation is similar to a luxury hostel. One family room has 7 single beds. A second family room has double beds, bunks and single beds to accommodate up to 12 people. Cots and high chairs are available. Visitors cook for themselves. There is a kitchen with a range that provides constant hot water and heats radiators. A variety of vegetarian and vegan food and home grown produce is provided, which is included in the cost of the stay.

The sitting room and dining room both have open fires. There is a playroom and garden, both well equipped with toys. All visitors are welcome to use the house and its facilities freely during their stay. Visitors are asked to respect other women's lifestyles. All bedding is provided. There is also use of walking boots and waterproofs.

Comment: One reader was grateful that such a centre existed. It allowed her and her daughter to enjoy their first holiday for some time. There was lots of fun and laughter in an informal atmosphere.

Sansbury Place Vegetarian Guest House
50 Duke Street, Settle
North Yorkshire, BD24 9AS
Tel: 01729 823840

Women friendly guesthouse. Two double, one single bedroom. Two guest bathrooms. Additional WC. Lounge/TV room. Open fire. Garden. Use of washing machine, iron, hairdryer and telephone on request. All special diets catered for. No smoking. Children over 5 years welcome. No pets. Electric blankets and hot water bottles. Parking. Closed last 3 weeks in January. Rates: £17.00 - £20.00 per person, per night. Brochure available.

Sansbury Place is a spacious, Victorian house run by Sue and Dave Stark. The two front bedrooms overlook the open fields around Settle and the rear double room has views of Ingleborough, one of the famous 'Three Peaks'.

Guests are welcomed with a pot of tea and home baking. As well as mouthwatering breakfasts, your hosts serve a 3-course evening meal, including wonderful dishes such as Mushroom and Walnut Paté, Flageolet with Juniper Soup, Autumn Casserole and Herb Dumplings, Asparagus and Peanut Strudel, followed by Lemon and Blackberry Charlotte or Hot Sticky Prune Cake with Fromage Frais.

Sue has extensive experience of running wholefood shops, teaching vegetarian cookery and catering for people on special diets. All food is vegetarian and carefully prepared using a wide variety of fresh, wholefood ingredients (organic where possible). Filtered water is used for drinks and food preparation and environmentally friendly products are used wherever possible. Tea, coffee and a wide range of herbal teas are always available and included in the tariff. The owners are willing to cater for personal special events, such as birthdays and anniversaries.

Settle provides a good base for exploring the Dales and Lakes. There is a wide range of places to visit, including Malham Cove, Ingleton Falls and White Scar Caves, Dent, Embsay Steam Railway, Bolton Abbey and Strid Wood Nature Trails. Visitors to the area can also enjoy a day out on the wonderful Settle-Carlisle Railway.

Grindale House
123 Eastgate
Pickering
North Yorkshire Y018 7DW
Tel: 01751 476636

**Woman run. House.   Four double bedrooms, two twin
bedrooms and one family room. Five of the rooms are en suite.
Tea and coffee making facilities, Colour TV, wine glasses,
toiletries and hairdryer. Lounge with open fire, TV and small
library. Garden. Washing machine and iron. One ground floor
bedroom is suitable for individuals who cannot manage stairs.
Children welcome. Pets welcome. No smoking in house. Rate:
Average £20.00 p/person, per night. Family suite at £17.50 p/p
per night. Open throughout the year. Brochure available.**

Grindale House is a listed 18th century town house, one of seven
terraced farms in the street. It is typical of the buildings in the area,
with its thick stone walls and red pantile roof. Situated in tree-lined
Eastgate, a short walk from central Pickering, it was the last town
farm in the area, with large numbers of cattle kept in the farm yard
at the rear of the building, until about 10 years ago.   The farm yard
is now a car park and garden. There is information at Grindale
House about its many interesting features and history.

Established as a bed and breakfast some 8 years, Grindale House
offers a friendly, relaxed atmosphere, antique furnishings and
antique beds.   Guests can enjoy staying in the individual country
style bedrooms, with modern bathrooms, TV and tea trays. There is
also a separate family room with 2 bedrooms and a bathroom. The
substantial breakfast is served in the farmhouse kitchen and
includes a vegetarian choice. Tuck in to yoghurt, fruit, free range
eggs, local mushroooms, tomatoes, sausages and home made jams.

Pickering is a small, pretty market town and is terminus of the
North Yorkshire Moors Steam Railway where you can buy a ticket
for the day and explore some of the loveliest parts of North
Yorkshire.   The railway runs special events for all ages and you
don't have to be a railway enthusiast to appreciate the beautiful
scenery as your train journeys through the heart of the North York
Moors National Park.

Kendal, Cumbria
Tel/fax: 01539 730340

**Women only. Self catering accommodation. One double
bedroom with washbasin. One small double bedroom.
Bathroom with toilet, washbasin, bath and shower over bath.
Lounge/dining room. Colour TV. Parking for one car. Fully
equipped kitchen, with washing machine and microwave.
Garden. Gas central heating. Bed linen and towels provided.
Sorry, the accommodation is not suitable for children or pets.
Open all year. Weekly rates on request. Short breaks from 3
nights also available.**

The self catering bungalow is situated in a quiet residential area on
the outskirts of the busy market town of Kendal, approximately 7
miles from the junction of the M6 motorway. Ideally placed for
exploring the Lake District with Windermere only 10 miles away.
The coast is easily accessible at Grange over Sands or Morecambe.
The town centre shops and restaurants, the leisure centre and
Brewery Arts Centre are 20-30 minutes walk, or a few minutes
drive.

Kendal has numerous closes leading off the main street, some of
them attractively restored to give the visitor a feel of what the place
was like in the 18th century when the wool weaving industry was at
its prime. You can hire a canoe for the day from Lakeland Canoes.
The large Webbs Garden centre (where the delicious lettuce came
from) has an abundance of plants, a good café and disabled access.

Visitors to Lake Windermere can take a trip on the Osprey, a silent
steam launch that provides one of the best ways to see the lake.
Alternatively, there are other more conventional sightseeing
launches that run cruises from Bowness Bay, Ambleside, Waterhead
and, at certain times of the season, from Newby Bridge.

Fawcett Mill Fields
Gaisgill, Tebay
Penrith
Cumbria CA10 3UB
Tel: 015396 24408
    015396 24060

Women owned and run. Converted mill. Full, partial and self-catering available. Conference and holiday centre. One family room, two double, seven twin and one single bedrooms. Two en suite bathrooms. Seven shared bathrooms. Tea and coffee making facilities. Use of washing machine, iron and telephone. Sitting room/lounge. TV room. Garden. Disabled travellers welcomed. Children welcome. Pets welcome. No smoking. Lunch, dinner, snacks and packed lunches available. Vegetarians and vegans catered for. Courses and workshops. Open all year. £16.00 -£20.00 per person per night. Brochure.

Open for 7 years, Fawcett Mill Fields has been lovingly and painstakingly restored by your hosts, Sue and Myfanwy (Van). Both are involved in the running of the mill and also lead some of the courses in their packed annual programme of events. Fawcett Mill Fields offers peaceful seclusion and is set in 3½ acres of meadow land with a stream flowing through it - and a waterfall! The meadow close by has a wonderful collection of wild flowers, some of which are rare, as the meadow has never been artificially fertilised. This beautiful countryside, midway between the Lakes and the Dales offers superb walking, biking and riding.

The mill has self catering accommodation that sleeps up to 21 people. The ground level is the Courtyard which sleeps 2-4 and above it, but separate, is The Mill House, which sleeps up to 12 people (minimum 6). The Stable Block can accommodate 5 people. The minimum stay is 2 nights. The stunning new group room provides an excellent environment for the various courses and workshops run at the mill. Courses include painting, decorating, gardening, circle dancing, yoga, walking, massage, psychodrama, astrology, gay gourmet and wine tasting weekends and advanced counselling skills.

Comment: Some really good courses in great surroundings.

Paula Day
Skadi Women's Walking Holidays
High Grassrigg Barn, Killington
Sedbergh, Cumbria   LA10 5EW
Tel: 015396 21188

**Women only. Three twin bedrooms. Two shower rooms.
Lounge. Garden. Sauna. No smoking in house. Dinner and
packed lunches. All food is vegetarian. Girls of 11 years plus
are welcome in the company of an adult. No pets. Open
February to November on specific dates. Prices start from
£155.00 for a 4-night/3 day walking holiday. Some bursaries
available. Brochure available.**

Paula has been running walking holidays for women from her own
home since 1987. High Grassrigg Barn is a stone barn with original
beams, which was converted in 1987 for its present owner. It is
beautifully situated in quiet sheep-farming countryside, with a
stunning view of the Howgill Fells from the main window. As it is
set between the Lake District and the Yorkshire Dales, a huge
variety of magnificent walking country is within reach.

The house is comfortably equipped for walkers. Guests can hire
walking boots and Goretex waterproofs. There are drying facilities
in the entrance lobby, central heating throughout, a sauna and two
showers to welcome you back and relax stiff muscles after the walk.
Evenings can be spent round the cosy wood-burning stove in the
sitting room and there's a gallery area with cushions and shelves of
books and women's music tapes you can borrow. On fine mornings
breakfast can be eaten outside on the terrace.

Paula's excellent home cooking is vegetarian and sometimes
includes ingredients from the garden. Fruit, biscuits and hot drinks
are always available. The bread is made with organic flour from the
local mill and the evening meal includes a bottle of organic wine.

Holidays are graded from 'gentle' valley walks to 'strenuous' hill
walks. Some have a specific theme, such as 'Garden Walks',
'Wildlife Walks' and 'Landscape Photography'.   The Skadi leaflet
gives full details of each holiday.

Apple Cottage
Near Brecon Beacons
(Easy access to Gower Coast)
Tel: Paula - 01269 824072

**Women only. Self catering cottage. One large double bedroom
with additional single bed. Private bathroom. Children
welcome. Pets welcome. Access to bedrooms may be difficult
for disabled travellers, but single sofa downstairs. Lounge.
Garden and patio area. TV in lounge. Open coal/log fire.
Central heating. Constant hot water. No meters. Parking.
Open throughout the year. Seasonal price variation. Discounts
for longer stays. Cost of cottage currently £25.00 per night or
£120.00 per week inclusive. Brochure available.**

Apple cottage is over 200 years old and situated close to Brecon
Beacons with easy access to the Gower Coast. It is a semi detached,
stone built cottage which has a welcoming open fire, a range and
well-equipped kitchen. It offers guests a comfortable and friendly
environment and is situated in lovely coastal and mountain
countryside.

The view from the front of the cottage is of a wide common used by
grazing sheep and cattle. There are also many horses which come
down from the mountain. Beyond the common and offering a
delightful backdrop, is the Black Mountain, this view can also be
enjoyed from the bedroom and front room. The views from the rear
rooms in the house are of the large, enclosed garden which is
colourful and well tended. The patio area has garden furniture.

Paula lives in the house next door to the cottage and, whilst she does
not usually provide meals for guest, she is happy to discuss
individual requirements. Bed linen and tea towels are provided.

Only 2 miles distant is the Brecon Beacons National Park. The best
views in the park occur mostly along the Offa's Dyke Path. The
Vale of Neath, with its magnificent and abundant waterfall area is
10 miles away. This area provides gentler forest walks in the
conifer plantations south of the Brecon Beacons, where waterfalls
and a series of attractive reservoirs are the main features. Swansea
City, which marks the start of the Gower Coast is about 13 miles.

Nr Llandysul
Ceredigion
West Wales
Tel: 01559 362 843

Women only. Farmhouse. One double bedroom. Shared bathroom. Tea and coffee making facilities. General access to washing machine, iron, hairdryer and telephone. Sitting room/lounge. TV room. Log fires. Garden. Lunch, dinner, snacks, packed lunches. Candlelit dinners. Organic produce. Home brew. Vegetarians catered for. No smoking in house. No children. No pets. Open all year. Courses. Discounts for longer stays. Willing to cater for special needs. £15.00 per person per night. Brochure available.

The farmhouse dates back to 1813 and retains many of its original features, including oak beams. Even the dairy, with its unusual slate sinks are still intact. From the bedroom you can enjoy the country views of green grass, trees, sheep, cows and free range hens. Organic vegetables, fresh herbs, free range eggs and some soft fruit are all utilised in food preparation.

Guests are welcome to make use of the extensive collection of books, music and video tapes during their stay. There are also bicycles for the more energetic. A bonus is the harpsichord, which musically inclined guests are welcome to play. Why not bring your own musical instrument for an impromptu music making evening?

The farmhouse is centrally located 10 miles from the seaside resorts of Newquay and Aberaeron. Collection is available from Carmathen train and National Express station for a small charge (to cover petrol). The surrounding area offers a huge number of activities and events, too many to mention - details available on request. There are photography workshops, suitable for all levels of photographer, including the absolute beginner. Each course is tailored to individual requirements. The delicious and wide variety of wild mushrooms found locally have prompted the development of further interest weekends in September and October, namely, 'Identifying and cooking with Wild Mushrooms'. You even get to eat your finds!

Comment: Friendly, informal and very interesting women.

Women Only Holidays/Retreat
Penralltwen, Cross Inn
Llandysul, Dyfed SA44 6LX

**Women only. Cottage B&B with one double bedroom
(accommodation shared with owners). Converted barn. Two
self catering caravans. Camping. Children welcome. No pets.
No smoking in caravans, cottage or barn. Rates: B&B - £10.00-
£15.00 per person per night; Barn - £120.00 -£150.00 per week;
Large caravan - £75.00 per week; Small caravan - £45.00 per
week ((both have nightly rate available); Camping - £2.50 per
person per night. German spoken. Leaflet available.**

This very private organic smallholding is an ideal retreat and is set
in 3 ½ acres of spectacular scenery of Ceredigion, on the west
coast of Wales,   The area encompasses Britain's first maritime
heritage coast with its breeding ground of porpoises, dolphins and
seals, as well as an abundance of other wildlife. There is a striking
and contrasting landscape which offers something for everyone who
loves nature. Your hosts can arrange guided walks or cycle tours
and there are also bikes for hire.

The converted barn is in a very private setting, with its own garden.
It has a wood burning stove, sleeping platform, kitchen and living
area. There is a bathroom, compost toilet and shower.

The large caravan sleeps up to 4 people and has a bathroom
compartment, the small caravan sleeps up to two people. There is
an outbuilding with a fridge, water tap and compost toilet.
Camping in the fields (not accessible by car) is ideal for anyone
wanting peace and quiet. The camp site has its own well, campfire
sweat lodge and and stream! There is an abundance of wildlife.

Marianne is a trained doctor and is now studying herbalism. Sandy
worked as a youth worker, specialising in outdoor education. Both
have a special interest in their large organic vegetable garden.

Local attractions include a centre for alternative technology,
horseriding, beautiful beaches, wildlife cruises to see the dolphins,
tea and craft shops, a dry ski slope, woolen mills, coastal paths,
mountains, and quiet lanes for cycling.

Chalet in Dyfed
Wales
Tel: 01559 371378

Woman run. Self catering chalet. One double bedroom. Shower room. Living room. TV. Kitchenette. Gas included. Electricity by meter. Rates: £75.00 per week July and August. Other times £65.00 per week. Open all year. Specific short breaks available at £30.00 per weekend. Brochure available.

A romantic, secluded chalet nestling in a woodland garden next to an ornamental pond with waterfall. Given its private and peaceful position, it is ideal for those women who want to get away from it all. There is a double bedroom and a living room with sofa bed and television. Cooking by calor gas is included in the price. The chalet is 1 mile from the nearest village, in a wooded valley midway between Carmarthen and Cardigan.

The valley of the river Teifi runs through this area and there are many old market towns along the banks. At Cenarth and at Cilgerran you can still see fishermen using traditional coracles. Each August a coracle regatta is held at Cilgerran, also worth visiting for the ruins of Cilgerran Castle, perched high upon a rocky spur above the river gorge.

Visitors to Lampeter can see St David's College or attend the horse fairs in May. Newcastle Emlyn has one of the last corn mills in the United Kingdom to use completely traditional methods of production. Visitors can see them all, plus a saw mill and museum, craft shops and trout ponds. On the west coast Cardigan's ancient bridge spans the Teifi and close by there is a castle, abbey ruins at St Dogmaels and a park of native wildlife. Also in this area is Aberystwyth, a resort and university town. Along this coastline visitors will find some of Britain's finest beaches.

Fishguard has an old fishing harbour, surrounded by small streets of terraced cottages. You can drive or walk up onto the high headland which protects the harbour.

Silverweed
Hanna Lindenberg
Parc-y-rhos
Cwmann, Lampeter
Dyfed, Wales SA48 8DZ
Tel: 01570 423254

Women and girls only. One double bedroom that can be taken as a single, twin or double. One shared bathroom. Lounge. Log fire. Use of fridge and tea coffee making facilities. Large garden. No smoking in house. Vegetarians and vegans catered for. No pets. Jewellery courses with individual tuition. English an German spoken. Rates: £10.00 - £15.00 per person per night. Open throughout the year. Brochure available.

This traditional cottage is built of local stone and slate and is more than 100 years old. It is situated 2 miles from Lampeter and approximately 25 miles from Aberystwyth and Carmarthen. Hanna is happy to arrange a pick-up service from Lampeter bus station.

The small cottage is simply furnished and Hanna is very welcoming. The bedroom is reached by very steep stairs which make the accommodation unsuitable for some guests. The room has a lovely view over green rolling hills and the Teifi valley. Guests can enjoy the large garden, with its lawn, flower and herb beds and pond.

Hanna lives economically and supports the notion of self-sufficiency, which is evident in her tasty vegetarian breakfast, home baked bread and use of home-grown produce wherever possible.

There is an interesting jeweller's workshop in the house and visitors can view a range of jewellery being made. Hanna runs a variety of weekend and week long courses, suitable for beginners and the more advanced. Individual tuition is available and participants work with copper, silver, gold and various gemstones.

Lampeter has a market that is worth a visit and also on the doorstep are the Cumbrian mountains. Within striking distance you'll find Brecon Beacons National Park (20 miles), Roman gold mines (8 miles) and a variety of beaches along the coast (16 miles).

West Wales Coast
Cardigan Bay - 9 miles
South of Aberystwyth, Wales
Tel: 01974 202231

Women only. House. Two double bedrooms. One shared bathroom. Tea and coffee making facilities. Lounge with TV. Use of hairdryer and iron on request. Garden. Children and pets by prior arrangement. Dinner and packed lunches available. Vegetarians and vegans catered for. Organic produce. Rates from £12.00 p/p, per night. Open all year.

Sue and Jill are pleased to welcome guests to their small but cosy home and will do all they can to make your stay a happy one. Situated in a village 9 miles south of Aberystwyth, the house is one half of a converted inn, built around 1840. It is easily accessible from Aberystwyth or Cardigan as it is on the main bus route. Food is all home made and Sue uses home grown produce picked fresh from her large organic vegetable garden. There is a mouthwatering selection of home made jams, pickles and chutneys for sale.

The sea and beach is 15 minutes walk away. There are many beach parties and barbecues held by local women's groups in the area, to which all are welcome. It is a wonderful area for walking, but if you prefer a different form of activity there are riding centres locally. The Monday market, operating in the village from May to October, is worth a visit. The village pub provides good food and local real ale. There is a post office and shops 50 yards from the house. Don't miss the enormous car boot sale held near the village on Sundays throughout the summer months.

Aberystwyth, a University town, with its sedate cliff railway, is within walking distance. It has the National Library of Wales which has exhibitions and collections of early manuscripts, pictures, music prints and drawings. At Ponterwyd is the Llywernog Silver Lead mine which has regular displays of silver panning, a museum, mine trail and underground tunnel with working water wheels.

Comment: A most warm and friendly couple. Great food, very comfortable bedroom and a bathroom with a lovely long bath with piping hot water! Well worth a visit.

Fachwen Ganol
Llwydiarth, Llangadfan
Nr Welshpool, Powys SY21 0QG
Tel: 01938 820 595

Women only vegetarian guesthouse. Double, twin and single rooms available. Other diets catered for where possible. Lunches, packed lunches and evening meals available. No smoking. Open throughout the year including Christmas and New Year's Eve. Rates from: £16.00 per night. Discounts for longer stays. Brochure available.

Fachwen Ganol is a guest house for women situated in the beautiful rolling hills of mid Wales. This 17th century longhouse has many oak beams, a lounge with an inglenook fireplace and log burner. It has 1½ acres of land, including a stream and ponds.

The house is secluded, has wonderful views and is set back from a minor road which is part of Glyndwr's Way (a long distance walking route). It is a very peaceful place with exceptional walking country, including miles of forest tracks.

A full cooked breakfast is provided and other meals are available on request. Guests are welcome to bring their own wine and can brew tea and coffee from a selection in the kitchen.

All the cooking is done on a Rayburn and where possible produce from the organic garden is used. The bread and preserves are homemade.   Convenience foods are not used. The eggs are provided by some very free range hens, ducks and geese.

Guests are welcome to make use of a wide selection of books, board games, O.S. maps, and tourist guides and leaflets.

The nearest railway station is Welshpool, 18 miles away and for those without cars a collection service is available at a small charge. There is also a National Express coach service to Welshpool.

Local places to visit include Lake Vyrnwy, Dyfnant Forest, Snowdonia National Park, Powis Castle, the West Coast and the Centre for Alternative Technology.

Dewis Cyfarfod
Llandderfel
Nr Bala
Gwynedd, LL23 7DR
Tel: 01678 530 243

Women only. Guest cottage. One double and one twin ground floor bedroom, each with en suite shower bathroom. Tea and coffee making facilities. TV, radio. Hairdryer. Licensed bar. Garden. Ample parking. No children. Pets by prior arrangement. Use of washing machine, iron, telephone on request. Other meals by arrangement. Vegetarian and special diets can be catered for. Courses. Discounts for longer stays. Open all year. Courses. Rates from £16.00 per person per night including full breakfast. Single person supplement. Discounts for longer stays. Brochure available.

Dewis Cyfarfod is a small, friendly licensed women's guest house. Originally 18th century cottages, now modernised, the name means 'the chosen meeting place'. The house, with its cosy lounge bar and the adjacent cottage are situated in an elevated position in 5 acres of woodland, overlooking the River Dee. Both guest bedrooms are situated in the cottage and breakfast can be served in your room or in the main house. All rooms have lovely views.

Art tuition is available at The Studio in Dewis Cyfarfod on an individual or group basis and can be booked in advance. Information about residential courses in calligraphy, drawing, painting, woodcarving, clay and plaster sculpture are also available on request.

Dewis Cyfarfod is situated on the edge of Snowdonia national Park. It is an ideal base for many leisure activities, details of which can be provided by the owners, who assure you of a warm welcome and a high standard of service throughout your visit.

Bala is a small market town, with a cinema and a choice of restaurants, bars and shops. Its leisure centre has a range of facilities including a large indoor swimming pool. There are also excellent facilities for canoeing, sailing, windsurfing, walking, fishing, mountain biking and birdwatching.

Shirley Risdon and Helen Varley
Kilantringan, Glenapp
Ballantrae   KA26 0PE
Tel: 01465 831211

Women run.   Self catering caravan.   One double and one single
(bunk) bedroom.   Private washroom.   Sitting area.   Gas fire.
Colour TV.   Mains electricity.   Car parking.   Using of washing
machine, iron, hairdryer on request.   No smoking in caravan.
Pets welcome.   Garden.   Open March to end October.   Bookings
from Saturday to Saturday.   Rates: £100.00 - £120.00 for
weekly rental.   Out of season overnight stays at £15.00 per night.
Brochure available.

Shirley and Helen gave up professional jobs to enjoy the 'good life'.
They are happy to give others thinking of opting out of the rat-race
the benefit of their experience. They have a small holding and
pottery studio.

Carrick, in the south of Ayrshire, is the place to find peace and
tranquillity in a beautiful rural location. The 24 ft comfortable
holiday caravan has its own private grassed area and parking space
and enjoys a lovely view. The surroundings are idyllic with a
wealth of wildlife. The caravan, situated in 3 acres of parkland
adjacent to Shirley and Helen's own pottery studio and small
holding is in a very quiet location and accommodates three people
generously. The dining area can be converted to an additional
double bed. One double duvet and one single sleeping bag is
provided. Whilst fully furnished and equipped, guests will need to
take further bed linen and tea towels. A car is essential.

Ballantrae (3 miles) is a small fishing village, with local shops for
immediate needs. Stranraer (13 miles south) and Girvan (17 miles
north) can be reached along delightful coastal roads and offer wider
shopping facilities. Cycle hire, sea fishing and a boat trip to the
famous Ailsa Craig can be arranged in Girvan. This little known
corner of Ayrshire has a wealth of attractions. Ayr is 38 miles up
the coast and Glasgow about 70 miles.

Kelvingrove Park
Glasgow
Tel: 0141 248 5219

Women only. Ground floor flat. One bedroom with double and single bed. One shared bathroom. Tea and coffee making facilities. TV. Use of washing machine, iron and telephone. Vegetarians and vegans can be catered for. Snacks by arrangement. No pets. No smoking in house. Open throughout the year. Rates: £16.00 - £20.00 per person per night.

The flat is on the ground floor of a listed building, built around 1850 in a road deservedly described as 'the most outstanding late classical terrace in Scotland'. The flats were built as town houses for managers from the shipyards whose families lived in large country houses.

The bedsitting room is spacious, light and south facing. There is a small double and a single bed. The bathroom is adjacent and is normally only shared with the owner. Breakfast can be provided in your room or you may join your host around the kitchen table.

The Terrace is quiet and safe but just off the main road, where there are plenty of buses and trains into town. The flat is 5 minutes from the M8.

Within easy reach are good cafes and restaurants to please every palate and purse, including film and gallery cafes, gay bars and various Italian, Indian, Chinese and Vegetarian restaurants. Even the city centre is only a 15 minutes walk away.

The city of Glasgow has exciting cultural festivals, radical arts, bars and events for minority interests. It has possibly the best range of shopping outside London, from the chic Princes Square to the Barras Market. On the doorstep are the Trossacks, Loch Lomond and the Ayrshire coast. It is a region of immense contrasts with some of the most splendid scenery in the world, which lends itself to those loving all kinds of outdoor pursuits.

Comment: The owner is very interesting and welcoming. The flat is comfortable and very well situated to explore Glasgow and beyond.

St Conan's Tower
Lochane
Argyll PA33 1AH
Tel: Sheena - 01838 200342

**Women run. Three self-catering apartments (details below).
Sitting room with TV. Fully fitted kitchen. Bathroom. Garden.
Telephone. Washing machine, iron. Laundry and drying room.
Welcome pack provided. No smoking in three of the
apartments. Packed lunches by arrangement. Children
welcome. No pets. Open all year. Rates seasonal and vary
according to apartment. Glen Orchy from £150.00 - £250.00 per
week, Cruachan from £180.00 - £280.00 per week and Ben Lui
from £200.00 to £300.00 per week. Brochure available.**

St Conan's Tower is on an historic site and is a tower house, built
around 1895 with granite from the local quarry. It is set in a
landscaped woodland garden which is a joy to see in the Spring,
with its spring flowers, rhododendrons and azaleas. There are old
pine and birch trees and rushing burn. Deer, badgers and foxes are
amongst the various animals that are frequent visitors to the garden.

Each apartment has a good, fully-fitted kitchen, with all facilities.
The sitting rooms have comfortable furniture and are well
appointed. Each has a TV and heating. Linen is provided. You
need only bring towels.

Glen Orchy can sleep two adults in the bedsitting room. Ben Lui
can sleep four adults or a family. Cruachan can sleep two adults in
a large double bedroom. Your holiday accommodation is set in a
woodland garden which enjoys peace, quiet and privacy. The views
are magnificent and overlook Loch Awe, Kilchurn Castle and the
mountains.

Jackie is an Historian and Sheena is a Horticulturalist and
gardener. They provide a friendly welcome with drinks in the
drawing room. They have a personal interest in geography, birdlife
and geology and can advise you on how to make the most of your
stay according to your interests. Scenic splendour, highland history,
hillwalks, climbing, birdwatching, traditional Scottish specialties
such as, seafood and good whisky, it's all here!

Scottish Highlands
Fort William
Tel: 01397 702267

Women only.   Two double bedrooms, one with en suite and one with private bathroom. TV. Tea and coffee making facilities. Use of washing machine, iron, hairdryer on request. Sitting room/lounge, conservatory and garden. Vegetarians catered for. Snacks and packed lunches available. No children. No pets. No smoking in house. Special activities - waterskiing and tuition. Open throughout the year. Rates: £12.00 - £16.00 per person per night. Advance booking essential.

The Schoolhouse is large detached house, beside a local primary school, but with it's own access and parking. The garden to the rear of the property is enclosed by a high wall and is totally private. The house is comfortably furnished and well equipped. The owners have a Golden Retriever and four feline friends - all having their own designated areas, unless friendly advances are invited by guests.

The house is situated in an area of outstanding natural beauty, surrounded by rivers, mountains and monuments. There are also wonderful forest walks. Glen Nevis has now become a film maker's paradise and was the setting for such films as 'Brave Heart' and 'Rob Roy'. Indeed, it is widely rumoured that Fort William has more mega stars on location than Hollywood!

Your hosts have their own tournament ski boat, moored on a local Loch and pre-arranged skiing is available, together with tuition if required. They are enthusiastic about the area in which they live and want to do all they can to ensure their guests have a really enjoyable holiday. A collection service is available from local bus and train stations. BR's sleeper service from Euston to Fort William is still in operation.

On the doorstep there is snow skiing at Nevis Range, hill walking, canoeing, etc. Horse riding and cycle hire is available locally. Visitors can enjoy day trips to Oban, Aviemore, Skye and Inverness.

Liz and Jill
47 Dudley Crescent
Edinburgh EH6 4QL
Tel: 0131 554 8179

Women only. Victorian terraced house. One double and one twin bedroom. One shared bathroom. Tea and coffee making facilities. Use of hairdryer and iron on request.. Dining room. Shared garden. No smoking. No children. No pets. Continental breakfast. Seasonal rates: £15.00 - £25.00 per person, per night.

This Victorian terraced house is situated in the Dudley Conservation area. The house is close to Newhaven village which has a number of excellent local pubs. Within walking distance is the Port of Leith, well known for fish restaurants and Sunday Brunch. The house is also in the heart of Edinburgh's gay area and is only 10 minutes by car to the city centre. It is an excellent base to stay during Scottish Gay Pride and the Edinburgh Festival.

Liz and Jill are two professional women with various interests and work experience. They enjoy meeting new people and have lots of local knowledge to help you make the most of your stay.

Part of Edinburgh's charm lies in the fact that in the 18th century the city's authorities decided to develop it. Instead of knocking down the narrow streets of largely mediaeval buildings in the Old Town, they created an entirely new part of the city.

The New Town is an absolute masterpiece of spacious Georgian town planning, stretching out below the steep crag of Castle Rock and is a pleasure to stroll through. It has been given great visual appeal by later additions in the classical style, columns and all. Most notably, the great neo-Greek temples at the foot of The Mound, climbing from the New Town to the Old, and the Doric colonnade, a prominent landmark at the tope of Calton Hill to the East.

Women Only B&B
Edinburgh
Tel: 0131 337 8087

Women only. Private house. One double bedroom. One shared bathroom with WC. Separate WC (also shared). Tea and coffee making facilities, Colour TV. Garden. Washing machine and iron available on request. Parking if requested. No children. No pets. Smoking in garden only. Vegetarian diets can be catered for. Closed Christmas and New Year. Rates for 1997: £15.00 per person per night.

The owner has welcomed guests for the past 7 years. Her modern 2-storey house is comfortable and welcoming and guests share facilities with the owner. The central heating is efficient and there is a constant supply of hot water for travel-weary guests. In the distance there are views of the Pentland Hills.

Food and facilities for a continental breakfast are left each morning for guests to cater for themselves - allowing guests plenty of flexibility and a lie-in!

The house is situated very close to Haymarket Station, approximately one mile west of Princes Street. It is very convenient for the city centre, public transport and all major visitor attractions.

Dunsany Bed and Breakfast
7 Gracepark Gardens
Drumcondra, Dublin 9
Tel: (01) 857 1362 or
Mobile: 088 69 50 51

Woman owned Three double and one twin bedrooms. Two bedrooms with en suite and two with shared bathroom. Sitting room with open fire and TV. Tea and coffee available all day. Telephone and iron. Pets welcome. Smoking in sitting room only. Vegetarian and vegan breakfast on request. Open throughout the year. Rates: £20.00 per person, per night. No single supplement. Brochure available.

The Dunsany is a 100 year old, red brick late Victorian guesthouse. It is an attractive building which has retained many of its original features, including fireplaces and stained glass windows. The house is beautifully situated in a cul de sac overlooking a bowling green and Maureen and Anne assure you of a warm welcome.

The guesthouse is 10 minutes from the city centre and guests can enjoy the hospitality of Dublin, starting with a delicious, full Irish breakfast at Dunsany that will set you up for the day.

Dublin City is a vibrant capital with many cultural and academic attractions, including Dublin Castle, Trinity College and Christchurch. There are museums, including the Dublin Writers Museum and art galleries. Dublin is also the home of literary geniuses and is the birthplace of George Bernard Shaw. The first home of Shaw's family is open to the public.

Dublin also has plenty of shopping and nightlife! The local hotels and inns provide Irish cabaret, music and dancing that will have you spellbound, clapping and foot tapping!

Other places to visit beyond the city centre include Malahide Castle, set in 250 acres of parkland, Newbridge House, a delightful 18th century manor in 350 acres of parkland, The Joyce Tower, one of a series of Martello Towers built to withstand an invasion by Napoleon, and Powerscourt House, Gardens and Waterfall, the location for films such as Henry V, Excalibur and Far and Away.

Mont Bretia B&B
Adrigole, Skibbereen
West Cork, Ireland
Tel: (UK direct) 00 353 28 33663

**Women run. Mostly women guests. Traditional Irish
Farmhouse. One family, three double bedrooms. Two shared
bathrooms. Sitting room/lounge. TV room. Garden. Tea and
coffee freely available. Candlelit dinners. Dinners. All food
vegetarian. Most other special diets catered for with advance
notice. Organic garden. No smoking in bedrooms. Children
welcome. Children's menu. Open throughout the year. Group
discounts. Rates: £15.00 per person, per night. Brochure
available.**

This traditional Irish farmhouse is over 130 years old and has
exposed beams and wood floors. The house has been renovated to a
modern but rustic standard to retain its character. There is an old
range in the living room and an open fire in the lounge.

The view from the bedrooms is of scenic rural countryside. It has
gained an excellent reputation, particularly in Ireland and the UK,
as a friendly place to get away from it all and really relax. It offers
comfort, good hospitality and excellent food.

All food prepared at Mont Bretia is vegetarian. Your hosts are
happy to cater for other dietary needs (eg vegan, coeliac, diabetic)
with advance notice. Wherever possible the food used is from the
organic garden and is cooked fresh each day. This good, healthy
food is accompanied by fresh, home baked bread. Your hosts want
you to enjoy your visit and have provided a wide selection of books
and videos for the use of guests during their stay. There are also
sun loungers in the garden for those chasing a tan. For walkers and
those wanting to explore the area round and about, guests are given
free maps and the free use of bicycles.

Mont Bretia is an ideal touring base for the scenic coastal area of
West Cork. There are a number of castles, stone circles and ancient
sites to visit, as well as beaches, cliff walks, forests and lakes.

Penny and Aine
Amazonia, Coast Road
Fountainstown, County Cork
Ireland
Tel: (Ireland) 021 831 115

Women only. Bungalow and self contained unit. One family, three double and one twin bedrooms. Open fire. Tea and coffee freely available. TV. Sitting room. Garden. Smoking in specific, limited areas only. Use of washing machine, hairdryer, telephone and iron on request. Partial access for disabled travellers. Children welcome. Pets welcome. Vegetarian dinner with home made wine and beer. Other special diets catered for. Closed Christmas. Rates: £15.00 per person, per night. Camping. Log hut. Brochure available.

There is a choice of accommodation. A bungalow, a luxury self-contained cottage, a log hut and a camping area. Individual enquiries will help guests decide which accommodation suits their need and availability. The accommodation offers guests privacy and great views across sea and countryside.

The airport and ferry port (from Swansea to Cork) are only 20 minutes drive. Aine or Penny will be pleased to collect you for a small charge. There is no charge for children under 6 years of age and a baby sitting service is available at £1.00 per hour.

Breakfast is vegetarian or an Irish fry - served between the convenient time of 9am to 12 noon, so guests can enjoy a lie-in. Earlier breakfasts, or breakfast in bed can be arranged with notice. Your hosts use home grown produce where possible.

Evening meals are served 5 days a week if required and you can be sure of ample portions of excellent vegetarian food, with the added bonus that it can washed down with home made wine or beer. There are also excellent pubs and restaurants nearby.

There is plenty to keep visitors active, if they so wish: kayaks, snorkelling, tennis and golf. At Amazonia there is a selection of equipment for guests to use during their stay free of charge. Reiki sessions are also available.

France, Belgium, Holland
Germany and Sweden

La Croix Cadio
22800 St Donan
Near St Brieve
Brittany
Tel: 02 96 73 81 22

Women only guesthouse. Three bedrooms. Lounge, Satellite TV room, telephone, washing machine, iron. Garden. Smoking permitted. Open April to end September. Rates 200 French Francs per room, per night, for single or double occupancy. Breakfast 20 FF per person. Leaflet available.

The owner is a retired teacher and offers her country house to guests so that they may enjoy great calm and rest. The old house is set in peaceful countryside and is very comfortable. It has central heating as well as an open fire. There is a lovely garden through which guests can wander.

For the musically-minded, guests are invited to play the electric organ, guitar, drums and piano. There is a library of women's books, mostly in French, but some in English.

Home grown fruits and vegetables are used in meal preparation.

Locally there are plenty of tourist areas and things to do, including swimming, riding and hiking. Nearby forests and lakes provide excellent scenery and countryside to explore and, of course, there is the Britanny coast with its good beaches.

La Maison Inanna
26340 Chastel Arnaud
France
Tel: 75 21 50 72

Women only. House and camping area. English speaking owners. Three double bedrooms. One shared bathroom. Garden. Patio. Bar. Children very welcome. Dogs £1.00 per day. No smoking inside house. Dinner. Special diets can be catered for. Children's menu. Nude sunbathing! Licensed. Closed mid September. House rates £17.00 - £20.00 per person, per night, including B&B and Dinner. Campsite, B&B and Dinner approximately £12.00 per person, per night. Please telephone for availability.

Centrally located between Paris, the French Riviera and the Alps, La Maison Inanna nestles in the Drôme valley and is an ideal area for your vacations in France. The house enjoys a secluded position on 5 acres of private land and yet is close to many exciting tourist spots and sporting places of interest. The double bedrooms are located outside the main house and have beautiful views over the mountains. They each have an outdoor patio with garden furniture.

In the evenings women gather around a communal table to enjoy home-cooked French cuisine. Special diets can be prepared, but prior notice will assist your hosts in providing you with a good choice of food. Dinner is served on the patio and it is an ideal setting for making friends, sharing sightseeing tips and planing outings. The evening often ends with dancing, laughter and talking late into the night. In a warm and friendly atmosphere, La Maison Inanna offers women an opportunity to meet new people and discover the French culture and countryside. For those with children there is a children's menu, play area and, nearby, good day care facilities, allowing adults time for themselves.

Visitors are well within reach of ancient towns and villages and château. In the Summer there are outdoor markets, craft fairs, festivals and concerts. The natural scenery is very beautiful and guests can go hiking, river swimming, kayaking and biking.

Jenny and Philippa
La Genévrière, Montgaillard 82120
Tarn et Garonne, France
Tel: 0033 563941381
UK Contact: Valerie Morton
Tel: 01225 862564

Women run house, plus gîte (available to rent separately or together). Separate B&B is also available at times. The house has two double and five twin bedrooms. One shared bathroom and four shared shower rooms. Four WC's. Sitting room/dining room. Fully equipped kitchen. Bar. TV room. Swimming pool. Garden. Washing machine, telephone and iron. Children welcome. Pets welcome at house (not at gîte). Smoking permitted. The gîte has one double and one twin bedrooms. One shower room. Sitting room/dining room. Fully equipped kitchen. Garden. Gîte open Mid September to Mid May and some other times depending on house rentals (used by owners when house is rented). Seasonal rates: House £555.00 - £1,175.00 per week. Gîte £80.00 per week. B&B at the house is £15.00 per person, per night. House open all year. Brochure.

La Genévrière is located in the heart of the picturesque and peaceful, flower award winning hamlet of Montgaillard, amid spectacular rolling countryside. The house is 5 km from the market town of Lavit de Lomagne and near to historic medieval attractions.

The charming and spacious house, with its spectacular gardens, is tastefully furnished and decorated to a high standard. It has everything for a relaxing and enjoyable holiday. There are games, toys, barbecues, racquets, hammocks, videos and ping pong. The kitchen is well equipped and includes a dishwasher, microwave, washing machine, freezer and food processor. If the house is not rented, it is used to provide B&B for singles, couples and groups.

The gîte has recently been converted and is tastefully furnished, with high beamed ceilings. The accommodation is bright and spacious with a large double bedroom. A selection of books, games, music and video cassettes are available for guests' use during their stay. A TV and VCR can be rented. The gîte has its own garden, patio, stone barbecue, hammock and garden furniture.

Marsès
11300 Fesles et St Andre
France
Tel: 003 346831 5773

Women only self catering cabin and camping. No smoking inside. No electricity. Rates: 100 FF for double occupancy per night and 70 FF for single occupancy per night. Camping 25 FF per person, per night. One week mountain tour is 2,000 FF including food and an overnight stay. Leaflet.

The cabin is situated in 20 acres of private land, in an area of peaceful seclusion, far from anywhere. The natural area is very varied, and has both a feel of the Mediterranean, with its dry, herb covered hills, as well as a lush greenness around the mountains. It is an ideal area for walking, mountain climbing and horseriding.

The cabin is of wood construction, built by the two women owners. It is small, but practically arranged with a kitchenette, a little woodstove and a double bed. A water tap and compost toilet are situated just outside the cabin. It nestles, completely hidden, in the forest and offers a romantic hide away for those who want to enjoy the feel of the natural wilderness. Treat it as your own private adventure holiday, or the opportunity for a meditative retreat.

The two owners, Regina and Adri, live on their land in a simple, close-to-nature way. They have a cat and horses to keep them company. They make their living by picking and selling the wild aromatical herbs that grow in the surroundings and by "transforming wool into warm and beautiful clothes". If guests would like to learn about wool fabrication - dyeing, felting and spinning, or about the medicinal and healing properties of plants the women would be more than pleased to share their knowledge and experience. In the Summer Regina and Adri run a one week, guided mountain tour in the high Pyrenees and would be pleased to take visitors who are interested.

Marsès is in the heart of the Cather area, with its special history and places of interest, like la Gîte of Carcassonne, the castle of Montsegur and the secret of the village of Reunes le Chateau. Also worth visiting are the hot springs of Reunes les Bains.

MONDÈS - House for Women
Courrensan
F-32330 Gondrin
South West France
Tel/Fax: (33) 56206 59 05

Women only farm, cottage, guesthouse caravan and campsite. Five double bedrooms in guesthouse. Private and shared bathrooms and a shower room. Sitting room. Bar. Garden. Washing machine and iron available. Children welcome. Pets welcome on campsite. Dinner and snacks available. No smoking in bedrooms. Open all year. Seasonal rates include a 3-course gourmet dinner: Double room is 165 - 180 FF per person, per night. Camping is 135 - 150 FF p/p per night. Camping only is 35 FF p/p per night. Brochure available.

Mondes is about 100 year old and set in the heart of the south west of France, in a lovely valley barely touched by tourism. There are fields of sunflowers as far as the eye can see, many medieval castles and grapevines from which the famous Armagnac is made. Mondes is a restored country house made of natural stone in the middle of 8 hectares of land, bordered by wild hedges and ancient trees. Courrensan, a small picturesque village of old, white stone houses is just within view across the miles of farm fields. Come for a relaxing vacation in surroundings created and enhanced entirely by women.

The large organic garden provides hearty vegetarian meals. If you wander outside you are likely to be greeted by any combination of the three friendly dogs, cats, ducks, chickens, sheep and two donkeys that live at Mondes with their owners! On the campsite is a small outbuilding with toilets, hot showers, a sink and refrigerator for your comfort and convenience. In summer at Mondes there is Standard Dancing on Thursday evenings, BBQ's and log fires and in the winter trips to the local pub for women.

You can just sit back and enjoy the hot days and starry summer nights at the farmhouse, or you may choose to wander off to enjoy the various amusements the region has to offer. If you are feeling energetic there is volleyball, badminton, ping pong and cycling. Alternatively, you may wish to visit untouched, small villages with characteristically medieval architecture, churches and museums.

R.I.F Roussa
F 32330 Courrensan
Tel: 562 06 58 96
Fax: 562 64 45 34

**Women only guesthouse and campsite. Six double and one single
bedrooms. One private and two shared bathrooms. Sitting
room, TV room. Fireplace. Garden. Washing machine, iron
and telephone available. Piano. Meeting room. No children.
Pets welcome. Smoking permitted. Dinner and snacks
available. All meals vegetarian. Closed during winter months.
Seasonal rates for half board per person, per night: 130 - 150
FF. Camping 30 FF per person. Brochure available.**

For the past 10 years this beautiful 200 year old renovated
farmhouse has been used to welcome women to a wonderful part of
south west France. Built of local stone the building retains its
original beams.   Situated in the heart of Gascony, Roussa can
provide comfortable accommodation for your holidays or weekends.

A renovated barn is now available for meetings and parties, where
group activities and courses of all sorts can be organised (ask for a
programme). There is a large park for sunbathing, a flower garden
and vegetable garden and an orchard, plus sheep, hens and cats!

The breakfast is a feast and the evening meal, including wine, is
tasty and nutritious. Home grown produce is used whenever
possible. Drinks and snacks are also available.

Sight seeing tours by mini bus can be arranged. You will find
several other women guesthouses in the neighbourhood of Roussa
where you can meet up for different activities. Every Thursday there
is a get-together at the market in a town nearby and a local
women-only disco every Saturday night during high season.

There is no mass tourism here, but you can still enjoy all holiday
facilities, such as, tennis, horseriding and swimming. There are
various lakes, including a small, private lake reserved for women. It
is also an area famous for its gastronomy, its vines and, of course,
its Armagnac. The area boasts medieval market places, roman
churches, castles, vineyards, corn and fields full of sunflowers.

Barrerie
Les Essards
16210 Chalais, France
Tel: (0033) 545986237 (France) or
(0031) 206002389 (Holland)

Women only. Campsite and apartments. Washing machine and telephone available. Licensed bar on site. Lunch, dinner, packed lunches and snacks available. Special diets catered for. Smoking permitted. Campsite May-Sept. Apartments open all year. Rates: Room 140 FF for double occupancy. Camping 40 FF per person. Breakfast is 30 FF. Brochure available.

Barrerie is a small, quiet campsite for women. There is room for a maximum of twenty people and it is open from May until the end of September. The campsite has toilets and hot showers. There is an outside fireplace and a licensed bar where guests can congregate and an outside terrace where guests can have breakfast and evening dinner.

There are also apartment rooms available all year. The apartments are made of attractive local stone and still have their original beams.

The garden contains flowers and herbs and guests are welcome to take cuttings.

Your host is a good cook and able to provide all meals if required. Home grown produce is used where possible. She is also a painter and enjoys sharing her skills with budding artists.

There are special event weeks, including walking weeks and tennis weeks. Locally visitors can enjoy canoeing, rowing, cycling, walking and tennis.

The campsite and apartments are situated in the south west of France, about 50 km south of the city of Angouleme in the Charente region. This area of France is still unspoilt and the climate is sunny and warm. Close to the campsite (6km), on the river Dronne is the historical village of Aubeterre.

Dagmar Bünemann,
'Saouis'
Cravencères
F-32110 Nogaro, France
Tel: France 62 08 56 06

Women only guesthouse and campsite. Guesthouse has two double bedrooms, lounge, TV room, garden and swimming pool. Smoking permitted.   Snacks and packed lunches available. Many meals are vegetarian oriented, but other diets catered for. Open April to November.   All rates include accommodation, breakfast and evening meal. Room 170 FF for double occupancy; 140 FF for hire of tent site. Brochure available.

Saouis lies in its own beautiful grounds, surrounded by sunflower fields, meadows and woods. It is approximately 50 miles from the Pyrenees, which you can see clearly from the house.

The farmhouse is typical of the type found in the South West of France. There are two double bedrooms in the house, two summer houses and a converted hen-house on the estate. There's also a lot of room for women to pitch their tents.

Dagmar, your guesthouse owner is a cordon bleu cook and you can be sure of some excellent food.   Most meals are vegetarian but Dagmar will offer meat and fish dishes, as well as delicious vegetables from her organic garden. Dagmar speaks French, German and English.   She likes dancing and music and invites guests to party around the pool during their stay - so you can swim or dance - or do both!

Your host wants your stay to be an enjoyable one and will welcome you with cut flowers in your room whenever possible. There is a piano, games, table tennis and information leaflets about the area and women's activities in the house.

Locally you can find monuments and churches to visit and there are markets operating every day in the little villages in the area. Toulouse and Bordeaux are approximately 135 km distance (about 2 hours by car). Much closer (within minutes) is tennis and riding. There is also a women's disco every Saturday night.

"Huize Vita"
Gieterijstraat 45, 8000 Brugge
Belgium
Tel: 050 34 25 93

**Women only bed and breakfast. One double room with
washbasin and shared bathroom. Tea making facilities in room.
No children. No pets. Use of iron and fridge possible. Car
parking on street. No smoking in house. Rates without
breakfast: 1400 francs for double occupancy per night and 700
francs for single occupancy per night. Breakfast is 150 francs.
Open all year. Brochure available.**

Huize Vita, or Vita's Room, was called after Vita Sackville-West,
the English lesbian who lived in Sissinghurst. It is situated only 10
minute walk from the city centre of Bruges and 20 km from the
coast.

Tea and coffee is served to guests on arrival, along with delicious
home baked cake. The bedroom is very English and very romantic.
The bed is made of brass and dates to early 1800. No male person
has ever slept in it!

Your friendly fun-loving hosts enjoy meeting new people and will
make you feel very welcome. They are happy to provide lots of
information on where to go and what to see in Bruges and can
recommend various eating places, including a vegetarian restaurant
minutes from the house.   If you would like to join them on
Thursday evenings, when they visit a lesbian café in Bruges, then
you will be very welcome.

Collection from the station can be arranged free of charge.

Women Only guesthouse
Sarphatistraat 119
1018 GB Amsterdam
Holland
Tel/Fax: (020) 627 40 06

Women only guesthouse. Three double, three twin, three single and one family bedrooms. One room has en suite bathroom. There is one private bathroom. Plus two shared bathrooms. TV and tea and coffee making facilities. Living room. Breakfast can be served at weekends if required. Kitchen facilities available for making drinks. No children. No pets. Smoking in living room and on balconies only. Open all year. Rates according to room size, start at fl 70.00 Brochure available.

Lilian's guesthouse provides lodging for women in a small, comfortable and personal environment in the heart of Amsterdam. You will be welcomed for short or extended visits. It is located in a renovated manor in the stately Plantegebuurt. Public transport is excellent and bus, tram and metro all stop within yards of the house. Transportation from Schiphol Airport is optional. There is limited parking available at the guesthouse and if required, parking requests must be made early. You may want to leave the car at home as Amsterdam lends itself particularly well to being discovered by bicycle and these are available for rent from Liliane.

Downtown cultural centres and a variety of nightlife and entertainment possibilities all lie within walking distance, for example, theatres, museums, concert halls, movies and galleries. Should you wish to attend a performance it is advisable to reserve seats in advance. Liliane will be pleased to assist you with this. A monthly entertainment guide is available.

Your room will be on one of two floors located directly above the owner's own home. To ensure that you receive personal attention in a warm, welcoming and comfortable environment, there are never more than nine guests. For your convenience there is a laundry service that will have your laundry ready within 24 hours.

The special events in the area include Queensday (April), Pink Saturday and Pink New Year.

Vaarschool Grietje
Prinsengracht t/o 187
1015 AZ Amsterdam
Holland
Tel/Fax: 020 625 91 05

Women only motor boat. Four sleeping berths. The facilities are basic but cosy. Maximum 4 women per trip. No smoking inside. All meals are available on a self catering basis. Rates: fl 345 for weekend, fl 650 for 5 days and fl 795 for 6 days. Brochure available.

The vessel Grietje is a former freighter. It is 54 ft (16m) long and has a width of 11½ ft (3.50m). There is a kitchen area, a living area and four sleeping berths. Learn how to maneouvre a motor vessel while you sail through the landscapes of France, Belgium and Holland. These are trips for the individualist and the nature lover.

Every morning a different view greets you as you experience the joy of seeing the different countries from the water! Every trip brings different attractions and goes to different places. For example, in North and South Holland and Utrecht there are quiet and beautiful waters, with old locks and bridges. Via the Zuidwillemsvaart you will sail through the beautiful areas of Bravant up to Maastritch. See the lovely countryside as you continue through the Belgium and French Ardennes to Charleville. Reims is reached via the beautiful Canal des Ardennes with its many typical 'peniche' locks.

There are opportunities to handle the ship, landing, departing and maneouvering through bridges, locks and tunnels. You will learn 'the rules of the water' and you will be able to receive a diploma on satisfactory completion of the course. The diploma is equal to the practical part of a Certificate of Competence.

Your experienced female skipper will ensure you feel at home even if you have never been on a motor boat before. This will be a holiday with a difference where you will have a unique opportunity to enjoy the teamwork and the spirit of adventure.

VrouwenBuiten Verblijf
Tolweg 38
9655 PG Oud-Annerveen
The Netherlands
Tel: (00 31) (0)598 491578

**Women only holiday resort. Three double, three twin, one
single and one family bedrooms. Three shared bathrooms and
three shower rooms. Sitting room. Bar. Washing machine,
telephone and iron available. Children welcome (special rates
apply - ask for details). Pets by prior arrangement. Smoking
in designated areas only. All meals available on request - mostly
vegetarian. Charges include breakfast, lunch and (vegetarian)
dinner. Open all year. Prices range frm Dfl 51,75 to Dfl 84,00.
A simple bed and breakfast rate is also available. Special rates
for women on low incomes. Brochure available.**

The Women's Country Home is a small guesthouse in a beautiful
country setting in the province of Drenthe. It can accommodate
thirteen guests and is a place for all women, to meet other women,
to follow a weekend course, to enjoy a holiday, or to work or study.
The beautiful scenery calls for hiking and cycling, while the nearby
river and lake has opportunities for canoeing and other water sports.

The bedrooms are light and airy, with plenty of windows offering
lovely views. The sitting room is very comfortable and has a
welcoming fire. There is also a piano, stereo and CD player for
guests enjoyment. Guests are usually impressed, both by the house
and the warm welcome from their hosts.

There are many courses and activities available throughout the year
including Watching and Drawing, Painting from Colour, Shiatsu
Massage, Canoeing and Sauna weekend, Women on Horseback
weekend and Servicing Your Bicycle. There is also a Summer
Week for Lesbians, an Autumn Week for Lesbians and a Spring
Week for Lesbians! Send for details of events and charges.

Nearby is a sauna and swimming pool. In the wider area there are
monuments, churches, rivers, markets, walks, riding, tennis, lakes
and woods. The lively town of Groningen is only 28 km. Here you
will find a variety of museums, restaurants, shops and bars.

Frauenpension Bertingen
Schulstrasse 16
25709 Kaiser-Willhelm-Koog/Nordsee
Germany
Tel: 0 48 56 495. Fax: 0 48 56 795

**Women only bed and breakfast, plus self catering apartment
and activity holiday. Six double, one twin and three single
bedrooms. Two en suite, one private and two shared bathrooms,
plus one shower room. Children welcome. Boy children only to
10 years of age. Baby sitting and children's menu. Pets in the
apartment only. Sitting room. TV room with Satellite TV.
Garden. Payphone. Washing machine and iron available on
request. Smoking permitted except at meal times. One sitting
room for non smokers. All meals available. Vegetarians catered
for. Rates: 50 DM per person including a breakfast buffet.
Approximately 15 DM if joining hosts for dinner. The
apartment is 90 DM for two persons, per night and 50 DM for
the servicing and cleaning at the end of the stay (see brochure).
Open mid Feb to Mid January. Brochure available in German.**

The rooms and apartment are in a large, old school house, built in
1886. It was used as a school until 1970 and has been run as bed
and breakfast accommodation by Christel and Lisa since 1990. The
school is a very calm, rural place to stay, but within driving distance
are lots of attractions, both in Hamburg and the small towns locally.

To ensure guests' every comfort, there are blazing log fires in the
winter time, video films, a fitness room, table tennis room, sauna
and bicycles. Good food is prepared using tomatoes and herbs from
the garden and local, farm fresh produce. There is often the smell
of delicious home baked cakes coming from the kitchen.

Guests are welcome to attend the Saturday night Barbecue, a weekly
event during the summer season. There is a slot machine for good
quality hot drinks. Also available, for the provision of alcoholic and
non-alcoholic drinks, is a self service fridge. Your hosts lead
guided walks along the "ground of the sea", very healthy but
potentially dangerous if you're not informed about it.
This house is a place for women who are able to enjoy silence, the
wind and, in the winter months, a rough climate.

Univiertel
Hamburg
Tel: (040) 453612

**Women only. One double bedroom. Shared bathroom. Use of
kitchen to prepare own breakfast. Tea and coffee making
facilities. Completely wheelchair accessible. No children. No
pets. Open Thursday night - Sunday morning and at other
times by special arrangement. Rates Dm 30.00 per person, per
night.**

The flat is situated in the university quarter, close to the city centre.
It is a modern sunny flat, and fully equipped for disabled women
travellers. It has a large bathroom, complete with bath with hoist
and a shower. The guest room is directly opposite the bathroom.

Hamburg is a lively city with many places for women - pubs, bars
and a weekly disco. The city also offers many concerts, exhibitions
and museums, as well as parks and beaches on the river Elbe.

Your host enjoys meeting new people and she will be more than
happy to spend some time with you, if that is your preference.
Equally she is happy to let you do your own thing. Do take
advantage of Marion's knowledge of the local area as she will be
more than pleased to assist you in planning your stay. If your
German is not fluent, Marion can either help you improve it, or use
her basic, but very adequate knowledge of English.

Hamburg is host to many special events, including the famous
Hamburger Dom; the annual Harbour Anniversary Celebration; the
annual Women's Ball, enjoyed by women from all over the world
and the annual lesbian and gay film festival.

The Northern Sea and Eastern Seas are about 1½ hours by car. The
famous heather landscape of Lüneburg can be easily reached within
the hour.

Frauenbildungshaus Anraf e.V.
Königsberger Str. 6
34549 Edertal-Anraff
Germany
Tel: 05621 3218
Fax: 05621 94726

**Women only farmhouse, self-catering apartment and campsite.
Two double, one twin, one single and four family bedrooms.
Two shared shower rooms. Sitting room. Garden. Use of
washing machine and telephone on request. Hairdryer.
Children welcome. Pets welcome on campsite only. No smoking
inside house. Dinner and packed lunches available on request.
All food is vegetarian and other diets can be catered for with
advance notice. Open all year. Rates: 25 DM per person, per
night. Food can be provided and a meal cooked for you for 20
DM. Brochure available in German.**

This traditional farmhouse (nearest largest town is Kassel) is over
120 years old and has exposed beams. As the former house of the
mayor, it is situated in the centre of the small and peaceful village.
There is a wonderful garden at the back of the farmhouse, which
can also be used as a camp site. Guests may use the kitchen
facilities and videos are available for guests to borrow during their
stay.

The farmhouse is situated in the valley of the small river Eder, near
a 25 km long lake. It is a beautiful place to walk in the woods or go
for a ride in the countryside. In the nearby town of Bad Wildurgen,
there is a swimming pool, sauna and cinema. There are a number
of stone circles, tombs and churches to visit.

During the summer you can enrol on the sailing courses taking
place on the nearby lake, the Endersee. At the farmhouse courses
on Shiatsu and Walking are offered. Shiatsu sessions are also
available. There is a popular summer camp for lesbians. Call or
write for details of each of the above.

Bikes and canoes can be hired in the village and sailing boats at the
lake. On Sunday evenings visitors can attend the regional
programme of events, including dancing and choir singing.

Artemisia Hotel
Brandenburgischestr. 18
10707 Berlin, Germany
Tel: 0049 30 873 8905
Fax: 0049 30 861 8653

Women only hotel. Two double bedrooms, four twin and two single bedrooms. Extra beds available. Six private bathrooms and one shared bathroom. Hairdryer and radio alarm in bedrooms. Sitting room, bar. Telephone in each room. One meeting room. Smoking permitted except during breakfast. Snacks available. Children welcome and able to stay free of charge until 8 years old if sharing female caretaker's/mother's room. Boy children accepted up to 14 years old only. No pets. Rates: double rooms 169 - 220 DM per night including breakfast. Single rooms 99-149 DM per night. Discounts for longer stays. Open all year. Brochure available showing the excellent decor, accommodation and conference facilities.

Established since 1989, the accommodation is easily reached by elevator and is located on the 4th and 5th floors of an older Berlin building. It is situated minutes from the Kurfurstendam, Berlin's most exciting avenue. Women's bars are just 10 minutes drive.

The hotel has been newly renovated and redecorated in soothing pastels and is very impressive. The hotel offers rooms with tasteful, modern furniture and facilities. There is a summer sun deck with a magnificent view of Berlin. Women travellers will find complete comfort and convenience and, whether for business or pleasure, the Artemisia's personal, women-identified atmosphere will make your stay a memorable experience.

Lavish buffet-style breakfast with eggs, cereal, fruits, vegetables, yoghurt, cheese, meats and jams. There is enough variety of choice to please everyone. Home grown produce is used where possible. A maid and laundry service available. There is adequate free parking on the street.

The house has changing art exhibitions by women artists on show in the bar, breakfast room and halls. Other paintings by women artists are displayed in each bedroom.

Kvinnohöjden
Storsund 90
S-781 94 Borlänge
Sweden
Tel: 46 243 223707

Women only farm, house, guesthouse, cottage and hostel.
Sixteen double, three twin, four single and two family rooms.
Seven shared bathrooms, 4 shower rooms and one sauna. Sitting
room. Garden. Telephone. Log fires. Smoking outside only.
Meals and cooking are shared by all guests and visitors.
Vegetarian meals only. Children welcome. Pets welcome. Open
May 1ˢᵗ to Mid August. Winter is for members only. Rates,
including meals, start from 165 swedish kroner for one guest
night. Courses Fri-Sun from 420 kr, and week long courses
from 1,750 kr. Send for postcard showing property.

Kvinnohöjden ('Women Heights'), is a none profit, women's
organisation that has operated for 15 years. The houses retain many
original features and are situated in an area of outstanding natural
beauty. The main house was built in the late 1800's and the oldest
log house was built in the late 1700's. Five of the houses are built
in a square, in a separate and seclude position up on a hill. The
property is surrounded by "very beautiful nature", deep in the heart
of Sweden and approximately 3½ hours drive from Stockholm.

In the summer different short courses are run (usually one week
duration) on a variety of subjects, eg building, printing on cloth,
photography, african dance, drumming, identifying mushrooms, etc.

Kvinnohöjden is an excellent base from which to discover Sweden
and is ideal for hiking, walking and canoeing. Just five minutes
from Kvinnohöjden is a beautiful lake where visitors can canoe,
row, swim and sunbathe privately. There is a wealth of beautiful,
deep forest in which you can hike.

One week is very special, where you can come and help build and
repair the properties. It attracts many women and is lots of fun.
Special music, workshops, plus a folk music festival in Falun, make
this a week to remember.

91

Spain, Italy and Malta

Cortijo El Peso, Apartado 13
Gaucin 29480
Prov. Malaga, Spain
Tel/Fax: (0034) 52 11 7041
Inside Spain: (95) 211 7041

Women friendly. Self catering. Three apartments (One twin, two doubles). Cottage with two double and one twin bedrooms. Swimming pool. Horseriding. Washing machine and iron. Dinner available at mainhouse by prior arrangement. Rates from: £220.00 per week. Winter and long stay discounts. Open throughout the year. Brochure available.

Hidden high in the mountains behind the Costa del Sol (½ hour from Estepona and the sea) lies the ideal retreat from the stresses of life. Cortijo El Peso is a 150 acre rural paradise ringed by mountains. There are well-mannered horses to ride and dogs, cats and poultry to complete the picture. Utterly private, your peace is punctuated only by the distant sounds of goat bells and cockerels crowing. Start dreaming of walks in wild flowers in spring, lazy days by the 20 metre swimming pool in summer and delicious tapas and a glass of vintage Rioja by the woodstove in winter.

Three self catering studious are ideal for couples or single people and an 800 year old stone cottage sleeps up to six. All are comfortably and thoughtfully furnished. There's even a welcome pack in the fridge for your first breakfast!

Gaucin has all the facilities for a holiday stay, including small supermarkets, various shops and restaurants, tapas bars and a bank. The village has fiestas during June and August/September, with a band, dancing in the streets until dawn and lively activities. Further afield, visitors can take trips to the Spanish riding school and sherry bodegas of Jerez, the spectacular gorge and winding Arab streets of Ronda, or the Mediterranean and Atlantic beaches. Seville, Cordoba and Granada are all about three hours drive from the farm.

Falcon Crest
33 Carib Playa
Marbella, Spain
Tel: 03452 83 83 67

Women only B&B villa. One double bedroom. One shared bathroom. Sitting room. Washing machine and iron available. Garden. Smoking outside only. No children. No pets. Rates from £15.00 per person, per night. Open all year. Brochure.

This large, luxury villa is situated in a peaceful residential area on the beautiful Carib Playa, six miles from Marbella. It has two floors and lovely covered terraces to protect guests from the heat of the midday sun. It is situated very close to the sea and a gay beach, as well as a pretty harbour just two minutes along the beach.

There are doors leading from the guest bedroom on to the terraces and the garden. From the extensive sun-roof area you can view the other magnificent villas - which are not too close! You will also enjoy the spectacular views of the Mediterranean.

Guests are welcome to make use of all the villa's facilities and can help themselves to tea and coffee, as well as using the fridge to keep fresh any provisions they buy. There is a BBQ on Fridays.

Your host has a good sense of humour and looks forward to welcoming you. She provides warm hospitality in a relaxed atmosphere, good food, comfort and value for money. Car parking is available and car hire can readily be arranged for you for collection at the airport.

The villa is conveniently located for visits to the old towns and markets. The area also offers pleasant walks and there are riding stables, a pool, golf and tennis courts nearby. The coast itself is very beautiful and there are numerous little beaches where you can swim and picnic in peace and safety.

Places of interest include Puerto Banus, a breathtaking harbour where million dollar yachts lie at anchor, Ronda, a mountain city and the colourful, unique town of Mijas. Further afield you can journey to Algercirus and cross to Africa for a day's visit!

The Spanish Experience
Malaga, Spain
Tel: 0181 697 7044 (Sarah or Susan)

Women only villa/hotel. Three double, two twin and one single bedrooms. One en suite, one private and two shared bathrooms. One shower room. Tea and coffee making facilities. Sitting room. Bar. Garden. Swimming Pool. No children. No pets. No smoking in bedrooms or dining room. All meals available if required. Vegetarians can be catered for. Seasonal rates per week, including breakfast and airport collection: Off peak £150.00 per person, high season £190.00 per person, per week. Discounts for groups and winter lets. Brochure available.

This special holiday not only puts women first by providing a safe and tranquil retreat, it is in one of the best situations in Andalucia, with its ideal climate averaging 325 days of sunshine.

The villa is situated in the foothills of Sierra de Mijas, overlooking the Mediterranean, with acres of its own grounds for you to explore. The swimming pool, totally secluded, is set in the midst of umbrella pines, with a bar and barbecue facilities. There are terraces with magnificent views towards Gibraltar, and the coast of Africa.

The accommodation, arranged around an inner patio with fountain, offers comfortable bedrooms, dining areas both inside and out on the terrace and a spacious lounge with bar. Good food, including an imaginative vegetarian menu, is an essential part of any holiday and your hosts give this high priority, taking full advantage of the abundant supply of locally grown, organic produce.

Courses and workshops are run here, eg healing, creative writing, walking and Andalucian culture - ask for details. There is also a good selection of books and music for you to enjoy during your stay.

Within walking distance is the delightful village of Mijas, noted for its white houses, its donkeys and wonderful mountain air. It is just a short distance to the beaches and night life of the Costa del Sol resorts, allowing you the best of both worlds. In the vicinity are golf courses, tennis courts, horse riding, hill walks, a gym and watersports at the local beaches.

PJ's
37 Carrer Major
07580 Capdepera
Mallorca, Spain
Tel: 00 3471 564427

Women run. B&B and self catering accommodation. The B&B offers two double bedrooms and shared bathroom. Self catering offers two double bedrooms, sitting room, kitchen, bathroom and private terrace. Brochure available.

PJ's is a large 17th century corner house on the road to the town's ruined castle, on the southern edge of Capdepera, an ancient fortress town built mainly in the 14th century.

Pam and Jane operate a wine and cocktail bar on the ground floor. The bar extends through to a bright and sunny terrace at the back, with the most stunning views of the outskirts of the village, the valley below and the mountains beyond. Pam and Jane describe this part of Mallorca as a special and tranquil place, with exceptionally friendly and outgoing local Mallorquin people.

There is a choice of accommodation. Two comfortable double bedrooms, offered on a bed and breakfast basis, or if you wish to look after yourself, a spacious apartment. Car hire is fairly essential and Pam and Jane will hire a car on your behalf at very good rates, for collection at the airport.

Capdepera has a lively market on Wednesday. The area offers much for the active visitor, with new golf courses, spectacular caves, ancient monasteries and a huge choice of sandy beaches. Additional watersports and other sports, such as tennis, are available at Cala Ratjada, a nearby fishing village.

CA NA NOFRETA
Asociacion de Cultura
c/o Christiane von Lengerke
Apartado de Correos 12
07570 ARTA, Mallorca
Tel/Fax: 00 3471/835023

Women only finca/guesthouse, registered society. The house has two double and three single bedrooms. (Finca details below). Lounge with open log fire. Vast grounds. Telephone, washing machine and iron. All meals available, including packed lunches. No smoking in house. No children. No pets. Rates: Pesetas 3.500 per person per unit. Prices for meals on request. Closed December and January.

Christiane and her partner have been running this guesthouse for the association for the past 9 years. Their regular courses for groups (5-7 in size) and self-organised groups take advantage of the facilities of the two houses. The larger house has one double and two single bedrooms and shower room. The smaller house has one double and one single room, kitchen and shower room. The latter house is let to women travelling individually. The finca is approximately 2 km from Arta and set in its own grounds of some 25000 square metres. It was built in 1984, using local stone, on the grounds of a 200 year old Mallorcan-style farmhouse. The rooms and walls of the house play host to exhibitions of paintings, photography and jewellery of women artists.

Both houses offer self-catering facilities, those of the larger house are shared with the owners. Some of the bedrooms lead on to terraces with wonderful views of Arta, almond and olive trees. For hot days there is also an open air shower in the garden.

Christiane enjoys sharing her interest in literature and archeology with her guests. She knows much about magic places to visit and the island's culture and history. Gabrielle, is a singer with a passion for classical music. The women love using home-grown produce in their new recipes - such as orange and lemon marmalade, fig chutney, figs in cognac and hierbas. It may be well worth staying for one of their special dinners, especially as there are good wines always available.

Casa Scala
Loc. Riletto 9
57034 Marina di Campo
Island of Elba, Italy
Tel/Fax: 0565 977777

**Women only house with four apartments. Six double bedrooms,
with two private and two shared bathrooms. Sitting room.
Garden. TV/Video. The apartments have kitchen facilities and
a fridge. Smoking permitted. Children welcome. Boy children
not permitted after 10 years of age. Play area. No pets. Closed
November to February. Open Christmas. Rates are seasonal
from 30,000 to 40,000 Lire per week. Single nights available for
women from overseas. Brochure available.**

Casa Scala is an old Tuscany landhouse with garden, situated 100
metres from a sandy beach. This small, Italian house with four
apartments and two sun terraces is surrounded by a garden with
trees and flowers and has views of the hills.

The apartments have a TV and VCR and a video library. There is
also a meeting room at the house and various workshops are offered
here - ask for details for cost and availability.

Car is the best transportation, but it is possible to get a train to Elba.
Guests can arrange to be collected from the bus station at Marina di
Campo. A bike can be hired for the duration of your stay at Casa
Scala for a small fee.

Your hosts, Marianne and Elvira speak German, Italian and
English.

The Island of Elba is covered with lush vegetation, such as wild
rosemary, anise, blackberries, grapes, cactus and trees as varied as
apricot, lemon, almond, pine, fir eucalyptus, cypress and palm.

There is much to be enjoyed here, including the local walks,
markets, the wonderful landscape, pleasant villages and sports
centres. Various boat excursions are available, including to some
of the caverns that are accessible only by sea. In July there is the
enjoyable, week long festival for improvised music.

Moria Deguara B&B
39 Pretty Bay
B'Bugia
Malta BBG 02
Tel (356) 651150

Woman run bed and breakfast. Four bedrooms, each with shower. Lounge, with fan.   Children welcome. No pets. Smoking permitted. Snacks available if required. Open throughout the year. Rates 4.00 Maltese pounds per person per night. Brochure available.

Moria's bed and breakfast has been established 10 years. She is a housewife who enjoys meeting new people and likes helping her guests make the most of their holiday.

The guesthouse is situated on the sea front close to a sandy beach and safe swimming. There are three twin bedded rooms and a family room containing three single beds. The rooms are simply furnished and each has a washbasin and shower.

Maria offers a babysitting service for women with children. Collection from the airport can also be arranged. An international telephone kiosk is situated outside the Motel. A laundry facility is available in the motel at a modest charge.

Malta is steeped in history and the prehistoric temples at Hagar Qim, at Mnajdra and others in Malta are amongst the world's most impressive monuments. Radiocarbon tests indicate that they are over 5000 years old and are the earliest free-standing monuments of stone in the world.

Locally there are plenty of bars, restaurants and places to visit. Throughout the island there is a wide choice of markets, museums, cathedrals, churches, grottos, lagoons and visitors will not be short of things to do.

India

NAARI, House No. 6130
Sector C-6, Vasant Kunj
New Delhi 110070, India
Tel: 00 91 11 646 5711
or 00 91 11 647 2114
Tel/Fax: 00 91 11 618 7401
or 00 91 11 623 4621

Women only guesthouse. Two double/twin bedrooms. One en suite and one shared bathroom. Lounge area with TV/VCR. Hot and cold showers. Ceiling fans and air cooled rooms. Hairdryer. Two small terraced gardens. Laundering service available. Girl children over 6 years and boy children 6-12 years welcome. No pets. Breakfast and other meals available by arrangement. Vegetarians catered for. Some disability access. Smoking in bedrooms but not in communal areas. Other meals available on request. Special diets can be catered for with advance notice. Open all year. Seasonal prices between 400 and 600 rupees p/p per night. Brochure available.

NAARI is the first women's guesthouse in India. It is located in an upmarket and safe area of South Delhi, in pleasant surroundings, within easy reach of the airport and city centre. This spacious, modern building has stone floors, plenty of light and indoor and outdoor plants. The women-run business can offer accommodation, tours and personalised tours around the city. If you would also like to be accompanied to the local market places where prices are low, and help to shop for bargains, this can easily be arranged.

Each of the NAARI rooms are tastefully decorated in simple, ethnic design and furnished to give a special character. During the day guests can choose to lounge outside in private, sunny garden or relax in the evening in the spacious sitting room.

NAARI is a great base from which to explore the sights and sounds of a new and exciting culture, without overspending in time, energy and money. To help you enjoy your stay at NAARI, you can request: candlelit dinners (which you can eat inside or out); a BBQ and holistic massage. Your host is an artist, as well as a mughlat, indian and continental cook.

Canada and USA

Wild Women Expeditions
Box 145, Station B
Sudbury, Ontario P3E4NS
Canada
Tel: (705) 866 1260

**Women only. Outdoor adventure. Private and semi private
riverside cabins and campsite. Wilderness and canoe/paddle
trips. No smoking inside buildings. Lunch, dinner, snacks and
packed lunches available. Special diets can be catered for.
Open 1st June to October 30th. Rates for canoe trips include
accommodation, meals, guides and equipment: 3 night events
approx. $150.00, 4 night events approx $200.00, 7 night events
approx $320..00 - $400.00. Rates for cabins, including 3 meals,
use of property and equipment is approximately $40.00 per day.
Some overnight stays possible - ask for details. Brochure.**

Now entering its sixth season, Wild Women Expeditions offers
women canoeing and paddle adventures and outdoor programmes in
northern Ontario and the opportunity to be in the wilderness with
the camaraderie of other women. For the 3 - 7 day wilderness canoe
trips you only need your sleeping bag, clothes and personal items.
Included in the price are the services of an experienced guide, the
required permits, all necessary equipment (canoes, paddles, life
jackets, tents and transportation from base camp to trip destination)
and delicious food.

If you prefer to stay at the home base camp, your stay includes
shared cabin accommodation, delicious vegetarian meals, using
produce from the base camp's organic vegetable garden wherever
possible, daily use of canoes and evening saunas in the Finnish
sauna. All this in 200 private acres of forest, meadow, hills and
wetlands, with many kilometres of river and creek, for guests to
explore on foot, or by canoe or rowboat.. For your benefit there is a
massage or shiatsu therapist available on site, by appointment.

In addition to canoe trips, there are events at the base camp on
themes exploring the arts and spirituality, including painting,
drawing, mask making, dance and drama.

Catnaps 1892 Downtown Guesthouse
Toronto, Ontario
Tel: (416) 968 2323
Fax: (416) 413 0485
Toll free: 1800 205 3694 (Canada, USA only)
E-mail: catnaps@onramp.ca

Woman run. Seven double and two single bedrooms. One bedroom is en suite. Two shared bathrooms. Lounge. TV room. Telephone, washing machine, iron. Fireplace. Air Conditioning. Garden. Sun deck. Parking. Children welcome by prior arrangement. No pets. Smoking permitted. Special diets can be catered for with advance notice. Rates: $45.00 - $65.00. For holiday weekends at $10.00 per night. Two night minimum stay May to October. Open throughout the year. Brochure available.

Described in its leaflet as "a traveller's home away from home", Catnaps has been voted Toronto's best Bed and Breakfast by NOW magazine.

All bedrooms have ceiling fans, TV and air conditioning. Breakfast consists of an expanded freshly baked continental breakfast and home grown produce is used when in season. There is a sundeck and porches for guests who want to relax.

Catnaps has been established 16 years and is situated in downtown Toronto. It is within walking distance of gay bars and gay village, the Eaton Centre, the CN Tower, theatres, Toronto Islands, Allan Gardens, art galleries, the university and Chinatown.

Your host provides free tourist information, brochures and maps so that you can make the most of your visit to Toronto. There is off street parking for a small charge, and laundry and maid service is available on request.

Woodswomen Inc
25 West Diamond Lake Road
Minneapolis
Minnesota 55419
Tel: (612) 822 3809
Fax: (612) 822 3814

Women's Activity Holidays. Operates throughout the year. Comprehensive brochure available.

Woodswomen has been running activity holidays for women, to a variety of international 'wilderness' destinations for 20 years.

You can rely on the group leaders' planning and leadership skills take you safely on a journey through some of the world's most beautiful environments. The experienced guides will provide you with the information and support you need to participate in wide variety of healthy and fun outdoor activities.

As part of the Woodswomen team you will enhance your knowledge of wildlife, ecology, geology and other aspects of natural history and you will improve your travelling and outdoor living skills. You will explore the cultures of faraway countries, experience beautiful, natural environments and get to know a small group of interesting, active travellers. The pace is flexible and group interaction is easy.

Depending on the trip you choose, you will stay in country inns, hotels, rustic cabins, haciendas, campgrounds or wilderness locations. Food will be plentiful and delicious whether enjoyed in the best local restaurants or the great outdoors.

Examples of trips: Dog sledding in the wilderness of northern Minnesota; Cross-country skiing in a Minneapolis park; Exploring the Galapagos Islands; Exploring Costa Rica; New Zealand Bicycle Tour; Cycling Hawaii; San Juan Sea Kayaking; Rainbow Island Retreat and Canoe Weekend; Mountaineering and Glacier Travel; and a Grand Canyon Backpack.

Yellow Birch Farm
Young's Cove Road
Pembroke
MAINE 04666
Tel: (207) 726 5807

Women run. Farmhouse studio and cottage accommodation. Farmhouse studio, available year round, has queen-sized bed, wood-burning stove, skylights, private bath and private entrance. Cooking facilities available. Two-roomed, self-contained cottage offers seasonal accommodation (May-Sept). Bedroom contains queen-sized futon and bunk beds. Fully equipped kitchen, woodstove and outdoor hot shower and private outhouse.   Children welcome. No pets. Smoking outside only. B&B $45.00 per night (double occupancy). Cottage $250.00 per week (double occupancy). Brochure available.

Yellow Birch Farm is a working farm situated on the coast of Maine, 30 miles from the Canadian (New Brunswick) border.   It is near the shores of wild, unspoiled Cobscook Bay, on a peninsula where you can hike, bike, canoe or kayak. The farm is almost 200 years old and constructed with original post and beam.

On the farm the women grow and market organic vegetables and make maple syrup and balsam wreaths. Bunny is famous for her breakfasts and Gretchen drives a team of oxen. Guests can pick wild blueberries, visit the farm animals and treat themselves to nest-fresh eggs and organic vegetables.

The Studio has a TV, fridge and hotplate. The Cottage is fully equipped for comfortable self-catering.

This is the perfect refuge for those seeking to escape back to nature. Much of the pristine seacoast near the farm is protected by the Moosehorn National Wildlife Refuge and is a bird watcher's paradise.   Moosehorn is inhabited by 216 species of bird, plus moose, deer, bear, beaver, mink and woodchuck. Some 50 miles of roads and trails are open to hikers. Visitors can also go whale-watching, explore the Passamaquoddy Indian museum, eat lobster on the wharf in Lubec, or visit the East Quoddy lighthouse on Campobello Island.

Lamb's Mill Inn
RR1 Box 676 Lamb's Mill Road
Naples, MAINE 04055
Tel: (207) 693 6253
E-mail: lambsmill@aol.com

Women run Inn. Six double bedrooms, with private bathroom. TV, fridge, hairdryers, toiletries in bedrooms. Lounge, two dining rooms, garden, telephone. Hot tub. 40 ft deck for outside breakfast dining. Children over 12 years welcome. No pets. Disabled travellers can be accommodated in ground floor room, but it is not wheelchair accessible. No smoking. Snacks available. Special diets catered for. Open all year. Room rates for double occupancy from $75.00, including full country breakfast. Discounts available. Brochure on request.

Built in the 1800's, this farmhouse has been renovated using original beams. There is a 3 storey-barn, original pumpkin pine floors and granite foundation. The fireplaces are constructed from stone found on the property.

You will be welcomed by fresh cut flowers in your room and can immediately enjoy the privacy and scenic views over the 20 acres of woods and fields. Your hosts invite you to sleep in the romantic atmosphere of one of the six bedrooms and awake to the aroma of a full country breakfast.

The Inn boasts 2 large gardens, herb garden, strawberry patch and apple trees. Walk in the gardens or take a leisurely stroll to the charming village, or nearby lake. The Inn is only 2 miles from a State park where you can swim in the summer and cross-country and alpine ski in the winter.

One women is an artist and the other a psychologist/therapist. Both are photographers, gardeners and avid outdoor activists and invite you to hike, bike, ski or boat. There is lots to do! Enjoy fishing, boating and swimming on 2 crystal clear lakes, browse through antique shops, go parasailing, aerial sightseeing, water-cycling, windsurfing or take a tour on the Songo River Queen. Play golf or tennis, visit the many country fairs and flea-markets and sample local Yankee recipes in small cafes.

The Highlands Inn
PO Box 118
Bethlehem
New Hampshire 03574
Tel: (603) 869 3978

**Women only Inn and Annexe, Farmhouse and Cottage.
The Inn has 20 guest rooms, a fireplaced living room and
wicker-filled screened porch. TV and VCR. Rates start from
$60.00 and include a deluxe, meat-free continental breakfast.
Heated swimming pool. Sunbathing deck. Video library. Hot
tub/whirlpool spa. Snow shoeing.
The Farmhouse, which has 5 guest rooms and a kitchen, is
available for individual or group rental which includes use of
kitchen facilities. Rates from $75.00.
The Cottage, which has its own TV/VCR, fridge, microwave and
sleeps up to 4 people. Rates start at $110.00. All bedrooms are
non-smoking, so an attractive smoking area is provided.
Children welcome. Pets in some rooms.
Murder mystery weekends, ski and golf package specials.
Lesbian commitment ceremonies, honeymoon packages.
Disabled travellers have access to 3 ground floor rooms.
Discounts for midweek and longer stays. Brochure available.**

The Highlands Inn is situated at the end of a country lane on a hill
overlooking its own 100 acres of woods and fields. It is surrounded
by the White Mountains. The 200 year old farmhouse was totally
renovated in 1983. Both the Inn and the local area has an
interesting history and your Innkeeper will be pleased to share it
with you.

All guest rooms are individually decorated with antiques and
comfortable furniture. The rooms have lovely views, good beds and
private bathrooms.

If your intention is to relax then you can enjoy the heated swimming
pool or the excellent video library. There is a piano which guests
may play and there is a good supply of books and games which
guest may enjoy during their stay.

Continued overleaf...

The Highlands Inn continued

For the more active, the Inn has miles of trails for hiking, bird watching, or cross-country skiing. There are lots of special events throughout the year and details are sent on request along with a brochure.

Your innkeeper wants to make you stay a memorable one and can advise you on how best to enjoy the wealth of activities, such as golf, downhill and country skiing, sleigh rides, tennis, ice skating, and horseback riding, all within easy reach. There are plenty of places of interest to visit including Franconia Notch State Park, Echo, Moore and Forest Lakes and Mount Washington Cog Railroad.

The Highlands Inn was the Winner of the Editor's Choice Award 1995-1996 in 'Out and About' Magazine, the premiere Gay and Lesbian travel magazine in the USA.

Bungay Jar Bed and Breakfast
PO Box 15, Eastern Valley Road
Franconia
New Hampshire 03580
Tel: (603) 823 7775
Fax: (603) 444 0100

Women friendly B&B Inn. Seven bedrooms, most with private bathrooms. Sitting room, fireplaces, library, private balconies, sauna, whirlpool, telephone. Spectacular landscaped garden. Children of school age only. No pets. No smoking. Snacks and Afternoon Tea available. All diets catered for. Room rates include breakfast and afternoon tea. General rates, based on 2 sharing, range between $75.00 and $150.00. These increase during Mid September and October. Brochure available.

The Bungay Jar is an 18th century English-style barn and was moved in 1967 to the present location in the Easton Valley overlooking the Kinsman Range of the White Mountains. It is a 3-diamond rated AAA establishment run by Kate Kerivan and husband Lee Strimbeck who particularly welcome women couples.

All rooms are exceptionally furnished and decorated, including antiques. The rooms have private balconies and soaking tubs and most have views of the mountains.

Guest rooms have welcoming touches including hand-made quilts, lavish linens, comfortable chairs and a desk. Each of the rooms have unique special features (eg The Stargazer Suite with its King size bed and four grand skylights for counting shooting stars while you fall asleep under mountain skies), details of which you will find in the brochure.

In the Winter you are welcomed by a crackling fire and the aroma of mulled cider and home-made snacks and, in the Summer, by Sun Tea or Lemonade and fragrant, woody breezes on one of the decks or in the garden. Help yourself to more than 20 varieties of tea anytime!

Continued overleaf...

Bungay Jar Bed and Breakfast continued

The widely-acclaimed garden, featured in magazines, defies description here (but we've seen the pictures and it looks amazing!). Welcome the morning by sitting outside on the deck, which overlooks the walled terrace, croquet lawn and water lily pond, watching the mist rise over the mountains while enjoying giant popovers, a bowl of melon balls and peaches and homemade granola, just part of the hearty country breakfast provided by your hosts.

The special events sound interesting and include a Lupin Festival and Frostbite Follies! Your hosts also arrange regular garden tours, talks and workshops.

Close to the White Mountains National Forest, Franconia Notch State Park and there are exceptional hiking, skiing and sightseeing opportunities. If you wish to travel further afield, Bungay Jar is 3 hours from Boston and 3 hours from Montreal, Canada.

Tin Roof Bed and Breakfast
PO Box 296
Hadley
Massachusetts 01035
Tel: (413) 586 8665

Women run and 95% women guests. Three double bedrooms. Lounge, garden, TV/VCR room, library, fridge, washing machine, iron, telephone, play area. Children welcome. No pets. No smoking inside. Open throughout the year. Rates $60.00 per room per night, with 2 nights minimum stay on weekends and holidays. Brochure available. Map sent with confirmation.

Tin roofing was popular in this area at the turn of the century and this farmhouse, built in 1909, has retained its original tin roof. The farmhouse has a front porch, with swing and a comfortable dining and living room area, complete with TV and VCR for the enjoyment of guests. Laundry facilities are also available.

You will find flowers and mints in your room on arrival and there is a good supply of literature about the local area. Your hosts want you to enjoy your stay and, having lived in the area for 20 years, can direct you to all the places of interest and the many activities available.

The garden has flower, vegetable, herb and water gardens and a lawn swing. There are spectacular views of the Berkshires and Holyoke range of mountains.

Breakfast is homemade (extended continental) and, as both women are avid gardeners, you are likely to be offered organic produce from their garden as well as fruit and veggie muffins.

Lady Jane's Inn
7 Central Street
Provincetown
Massachusetts 02657
Tel: (508) 487 3387
E-mail: LadyJanes@Wn.Net

Women run guesthouse, with a 99% women clientele. Ten bedrooms, all with private bathrooms. TV in bedrooms, plus ceiling fans. Lounge, with courtesy telephone. TV/VCR room. Limited disabled access. Pets with prior approval. No smoking in common areas. Room rates from $60.00 off season. Brochure available.

Constructed in 1986, Lady Jane's Inn is a women-owned and operated guesthouse. It is located in the heart of Provincetown on a quiet side of the street, but close to the excitement and activity of this popular resort town.

The Inn combines convenience and quality with the nostalgia and charm of days gone by. It has been carefully and tastefully designed for comfort, pleasure and privacy. All rooms are furnished with antiques and have individual heating and air-conditioning.

There is a common hospitality room where guests can enjoy TV/VCR, books, games and use of the fridge. Guests can also relax on the flower-filled outside patio.

The complimentary continental breakfast includes coffee and tea, juice and freshly baked muffins or breads.

Free parking on site is provided. Airport and boat pickup and departure can be arranged with prior notice.

To help you enjoy your stay the staff at Lady Jane's will assist guests in making arrangements for such activities as whale-watching, dune tours, boat rentals or horseback riding.

Rose Acre
5 Center Street
Provincetown
Massachusetts 02657
Tel: (508) 487 2347
E-mail: Roserugosa@aol.com

Women only guesthouse made up of 4 suites, also cottage for 2 people. All units have kitchens and private baths. Small rustic cottage on beach. Garden, sun area, Gas BBQ, cable TV and iron. Parking. No children. No pets. Smoking in ground floor units only. Open throughout the year. Off-season prices start at $65.00 per unit. Brochure available.

Rose Acre guest house has four suites, of various sizes accommodating 2, 3 or 4 people each. There is also a cottage for 2 people. The guest house is a rambling 1840 post and beam and shingled Cape House, tucked down a private drive in the centre of town. It was once the domain of a Portuguese fishing family and enjoys water views, the sound of the fog horn and the smell of salt air. There is a spacious private yard and garden which provide a pleasant place to relax, catch some sun and picnic.

All units have a private entrance, heat and cable TV. They are designed for self-catering comfort and come adorned with wicker, flowers and art, reflecting the fact that both women are artists. Carol and Rosemary are well travelled and have both relinquished careers in the academic world.

Also for rent is a 'Cabana for 2', described as a very small rustic cottage on the beach. It has inside plumbing and an outside shower. There is a TV, parking and a pool and is away from the main guest house.

Plums Bed & Breakfast Inn
160 Bradford Street
Provincetown
Massachusetts 02657
Tel: (508) 487 2283

Women only guesthouse. Five en-suite bedrooms. Common room with TV/VCR. Ceiling fans. Garden. Front porch. Parking. No smoking in house. No children. No pets. Vegetarians catered for. Closed January and February. Off-season prices start at $78.00 per room. Brochure available.

Plums is an 1860's Dutch Gambrel set inside a white picket fence, a garden of lilies, irises and dahlias. This was previously a Victorian whaling captain's house, with large rooms pleasantly graced with fresh flowers, lace curtains and Victorian antiques. There is a daily maid service for the convenience of guests.

For the past 14 years Plums has been catering for guests from around the world. Sit at a table of women and wait to be served with a full gourmet breakfast served daily in the common room. Wild cranberries from the bogs in the dunes and fresh herbs from the garden are used in baking. A variety of offerings including french toast stuffed with cream cheese and strawberries, entrees such as cheese soufflé and fresh fruit are part of the women's plan to pamper your taste buds.

One of your Innkeepers is a sculptor who uses flotsam from the beaches to create her art. The other woman is a poet and writer.

Your Innkeepers also rent condos throughout Provincetown and can provide details on request.

The Dusty Miller Inn
82 Bradford Street
Provincetown
Massachusetts 02657
Tel: (508) 487 2213

Women run Inn, motel and apartment with a 90% women clientele. Thirteen bedrooms, most with private bath and shower. Small fridge and coffee machines in most rooms. TV in some rooms. Sitting room, TV room, iron. Children welcome. Pets welcome in some rooms with prior arrangement. Smoking allowed. Closed in December. Room rates for double occupancy start at $45.00 off season. Brochure available.

The Dusty Miller Inn was built in the 1860's as a private residence and has been a guest house for the past 30 years. Carole, the present owner bought the inn in 1981 and named it the Dusty Miller Inn after the silver-leafed plant which grows wild on the dunes of Cape Cod. The Inn's front porch is perfect for friendly conversation and people-watching. Coffee and tea is served on the porch in the Summer

This friendly Inn is conveniently located near the centre of town and is within walking distance of everything in Provincetown, including its art galleries, shops, fine restaurants and bars.

The Inn rooms are comfortable and homey. Located on the first and second floor of the house they have a double bed and unique furnishings. The motel rooms are more self-contained and are located in the two-storey addition to the house. Each motel room is individually decorated, has a private entrance, double bed, fridge, cable TV and private bath.

The apartment has its own porch and private entrances. It has a bright living room, with futon sofa for extra sleeping accommodation, cable TV and a fully equipped kitchen. A narrow spiral staircase leads to a cosy bedroom with a double bed.

Bradford Gardens Inn
179 Bradford Street
Provincetown
Massachusetts 02657
Tel: (508) 487 1616

**Woman run guesthouse, cottage and townhouses. There are 18
rooms, including 7 family rooms, each with private bathroom.
Lounge, garden, telephone, iron. Fireplaces in most rooms.
Parking. TV and fridge in all rooms. Coffee-maker, toaster and
microwave in some rooms. Smoking in most guest rooms, but
not in common areas. Children welcome. Pets welcome off
season (Sept-May). Vegetarians catered for. Open throughout
the year. Daily rates start at $75.00 off-season. Brochure
available.**

Bradford Gardens is an 1820's Colonial Inn which offers true New
England hospitality, with all the convenience of a gracious country
home. Set in an acre of land it has beautiful gardens, featuring
cherry and fruit trees and rose bushes.

In the old Inn there are 8 rooms and apartments. Behind the Inn is
the large and unusual 'Loft Lodge' with two loft bedrooms, which
offers accommodation for 6 people. It includes a deck, patio,
fireplace and full kitchen. The 'Beloved Toad' is a cosy lodge with
one loft bedroom, sleeps 4 and has a full kitchen, unique corner
fireplace and patio off the rose garden.

All rooms are uniquely different in character, combining the charm
of real, working fireplaces and period furnishing with the modern
comfort of colour televisions and private bathrooms. Rooms are
decorated with fresh flowers and antiques and have scenic views.
Room rates include daily maid service, firewood, on-site parking
and full gourmet breakfast. The full list of accommodation can be
found in the brochure.

Breakfast is served in the Morning Room, with its central fireplace
and a large bay window overlooking the garden, which provides a
delightful setting for guests to mingle.

Geri Luongo
Club le Bon, PO Box 444
Woodbridge, New Jersey 07095
Tel/Fax: (908) 826 1577
E-mail: Clublebon@aol.com

Woman only resort holidays in the Caribbean and South America. Deluxe, all-inclusive, package tour holidays start at $899.00 per week per woman. Some special diets can be catered for. Many packages include airfare from within the USA - details on request. Brochures available.

Geri has been in the travel and tourism industry for 25 years and established Club le Bon 7 years ago. She specialises in women only deluxe resort holidays in high-class hotels in remote, secluded destinations. Geri also arranges lesbian and gay family holidays. For example, in 1997, 30 gay parents and their children will be enjoying a private family get-away at Isla Mujeres, Yucatan. This holiday is also available as a women only option.

An example of what you can expect is an exclusive 7-night, women only holiday in Barbados. You will stay in a small intimate resort on the east coast, featuring a secluded cove beach surrounded by dramatic rock formations.

Limited to 32 women, your holiday promises privacy, magnificent views, entertainment and much more. Your holiday price includes round-trip transfers, accommodation, a reception cocktail party, 3 meals daily, drinks to the value of $25.00, a gourmet dine-around, a day's Catamaran Sail with snorkelling, BBQ beach party, transportation to local events, dinner show, entertainment, farewell cocktail part and tips and taxes. Also available is massage, mini-moke rentals, horseback riding on the beach, shopping and snorkelling. Other optional sightseeing tours include, visits to a nature preserve, botanical gardens, cave tours deep sea fishing, surfing and diving.

Should you want to try something completely different, Geri also organises an Amazon Rain forest Riverboat Tour for a maximum of 18 women. This is a 6-night tour where your accommodation is on a deluxe, air-conditioned Riverboat. Details available on request.

Mary Ann and Julie
Honeysuckle
Milton
Delaware 19968
Tel: (302) 684 3284

Women only. Eight double bedrooms in total. Lounge, garden, TV room, cable TV, telephone, iron. Also swimming pool, hot tub and sauna. No children. No pets. Disabled travellers can be accommodated in ground floor suite, which has bath, kitchen and dining area. Some special diets catered for with advance notice. No smoking indoors. Open throughout year. Honeysuckle rates start at $80.00 per night for double occupancy. The weekly rates for Wisteria and Larkspur are currently $600.00 for 1-2 women and $800.00 for 3-4 women. Brochures available.

This establishment comprises: the main house, Honeysuckle, a Victorian Inn; Larkspur, an original Delaware farmhouse, which is behind the main house; and Wisteria, a charming Victorian house situated next to Honeysuckle.

Described as one of the most gracious Victorian homes in Milton, Delaware, Honeysuckle is a welcoming bed and breakfast with an easy-going atmosphere. It is the aim of the owners to provide a place where women can feel at home. In the winter you can enjoy hot chocolate by the fireplace, in the summer you can lounge by the pool. Privacy fencing allows a playful daytime splash or a sensuous moonlight dip.

Built around 1850, Honeysuckle is listed in the National Register of Historic Places. Guests have the "run of the house" and are welcome to use the grand piano, stereo, TV and VCR, the variety of games and library of women's books.   You can also use the kitchen after midday for your own cooking requirements and can help yourself to teas and coffee anytime.

To help you begin your day well, the women provide a variety of delicious breakfasts and, with advance notice, will cater for any food restrictions.

Continued overleaf...

Honeysuckle continued

Wisteria is self-catering and enables guests to enjoy their own space and consists of a living room, dining room, full kitchen, 2 bedrooms, 1½ baths, whirlpol tub and massage room. For guests individual comfort there is self-controlled heating and air-conditioning.

Larkspur, also self-catering, is an original 1820's Delaware farmhouse "found" in the middle of a cornfield by the current owners and moved to their yard behind the pool! It has been carefully re-modelled to create a very special, very cosy and private space for guests and their friends. It consists of a living room, dining area, small, full kitchen, 2 bedrooms, 1 bath and a sitting room with a game table, TV and VCR. It has self-controlled heating and air-conditioning.

Guests who stay in Wisteria or Larkspur are welcome to visit Honeysuckle and can use the Inn's pool, hot tub, sauna, outside shower and the downstairs common place to meet up with like-minded women.

In the surrounding area there are bay beaches, boardwalks, restaurants and night life. Activities include canoeing, hiking, fishing, tennis and bicycling. You can also take day trips to Delaware Bay by ferry, visit Atlantic City's casinos, see wild horses at Assateague Island or visit the Bombay Hook Nature preserve.

Above the Clouds Bed and Breakfast
North Georgia Mountains
Near Dahlonega, Georgia
Tel: (706) 864 5211

Woman only. Two double bedrooms with en-suite. Lounge, with TV/VCR, kitchen, telephone, washing machine, iron. Bedrooms have a coffee-making facility, TV, fridge and hairdryer. No children. Disabled travellers can be accommodated in one room which is totally wheelchair accessible, including the bath. Pets may be accommodated - please discuss in advance. Outside hot tub. Smoking outdoors only. Vegetarian and gluten-free diets catered for. Snacks and packed lunches available. Open all year. Room rates are $80.00 per night with 2 nights minimum stay. Weekly rates on request. Brochure available.

Built on a mountain side of cedar and mountain stone, near the site of the first gold rush, Above the Clouds is a quiet, private retreat for women travellers. Bedrooms are well equipped for guests' enjoyment, including the use of TV and VCR, tape and CD player, and complimentary coffee, tea and soft drinks. Both bedrooms have a deck for sunbathing and a glorious 50 mile view of the Appalachian Mountains.

Dahlonega is at the southern tip of the Blue Ridge Mountains and the Appalachian Trail crosses about two miles distance. It is a historic gold-mining village, where visitors can go on mine tours, pan for gold and visit the various mountain craft and antique shops around the square in the town centre.

The various activities in the local area are well illustrated in brochures available in your room, including opportunities to go antiques-hunting or day visits to waterfalls. Lake Dockery, a pleasant picnic and fishing spot is approximately 1 mile away.

There is a good choice of eating establishments in Dahlonega, including Southern BBQ, family style dining and a candlelit gourmet restaurant.

127

Swiftwaters
830 Swiftwaters Road
Dahlonega
Georgia 30533
Tel: (706) 864 3229

Woman only Bed and Breakfast, cabins and campground. Lounge, garden, washing machine, iron. Satellite TV. No children. Pets welcome. Smoking outdoors only. Most diet requirements can be managed with advance notice. Camping from $10.00 per woman per night. Other rates on request. Brochure available.

Swiftwaters is situated near the site of the first US Gold Rush in 1828. Dahlonega is the Cherokee word for gold and the town has a Gold Museum and mine that has been opened for tourists. There are quaint shops and good restaurants in the town square.

The bed and breakfast room has a separate entrance at one end of the women's home. It has its own bath, hot tub and dressing room. There is a small library of women's books, a coffee-maker and clock radio. The room has its own deck where you can sunbathe or use the charcoal grill. However, there is no kitchen facility.

If you are celebrating something special your hosts are happy to put some champagne on ice as their gift to your celebration.

The cabins are located on a hill close to the house but far enough away to afford some privacy. Each cabin is rustic, but has enough comforts to make your stay relaxing and enjoyable. The cabins are not heated. Breakfast can be arranged with advance notice and Joyce is known for her blueberry pancakes, which are made from homegrown blueberries!

The campground accommodates 70-100 women in 22 acres of meadow and wooded hills, surrounded by headwaters and mountain streams in the foothills of the Blue Ridge mountains.

There are plenty of opportunities to play volleyball, throw horseshoes, go tubing on the river or for guests to try horseback riding, hiking or whitewater canoeing or gold panning.

Pagoda
2854 A1A Coastal Highway
St Augustine
Florida
Tel: (904) 824 2970

Woman only hostel and cottages - a spiritual and cultural retreat. Five double bedrooms in total. Lounge, TV/VCR, washing machine, telephone for local calls only. Wheelchair accessible bedroom, efficiency kitchen, bath and grounds. Children if accompanied by responsible mothers - no specific amenities available. No pets. Smoking by rear pool area only. Open throughout the year. This is a vegetarian-only establishment. Reservations only. Rates $20.00 per woman per night. Brochure available.

Originally the home of the Timucuan people, St Augustine became the first and oldest European settlement in North America when it was founded by the Spanish over 400 years ago. This pretty town has a population of less than 12,000 and yet, as a tourist town, has many historical sites of interest, good beaches and an abundance of excellent restaurants.

Situated near the Old District of town, Pagoda is a quiet, simple retreat house within a 20 year-old established lesbian beach community. Guest bedrooms are private and simply furnished. Guests share the kitchen, which is for vegetarian use only, and bath facilities. There is a swimming pool for the use of the community women and guests.

Pagoda is an old, wooden beach house, complete with its own theatre, where it holds occasional concerts, events and circles. The main floor has a porch looking out onto the beach and the attic room has an ocean view. Guests can swim and lounge at the nudity-optional pool or on the beach, read a book from the Pagoda's library, or chat with like-minded women in the common areas.

Because the centre is a special, women's-only space, in the heart of a lesbian community, no males of any age may visit it.

Rainbow House
525 United Street
Key West
Florida 33040
Tel: (305) 292 1450

Woman only guest house. Twenty-five double bedrooms with private bath. All bedrooms have a TV, queen-size bed, air conditioning and ceiling fan. Some bedrooms have a fridge or kitchenette. Garden, swimming pool, telephone, iron. Hot tub. No children. No pets. Smoking outside only. Open throughout the year. Summer rates $69.00-$139.00 per room. Winter rates $99.00-$189.00 per room. Brochure available.

Situated at the southern-most tip of Florida on the island of Key West, this lesbian owned and operated guest house has been established 8 years. The balconied structure, with its clapboard exterior and deep porches, was erected in 1886 and has witnessed a small litany of women owners on its journey from cigar factory to guest house in 1990!

Guests at the Rainbow House can enjoy the swimming pool, the extensive decking for sunbathing and a shaded tropical pavillion for lazy-day lounging. It also has a slate covered, full size pool table. Conveniently situated for shops , restaurants, discos and clubs, Rainbow house is only 1 block from the Atlantic Ocean.

Start your day with an expanded continental breakfast, which can be enjoyed in the air-conditioned pavillion or by the pool. You can indulge yourself in a massage poolside or in the privacy of your room. Later in the evening why not slip into the outdoor hot-tub.

When you are ready to experience the rest of the island, with its reputation for being gay-friendly, the full time Concierge will help you plan snorkelling, scuba, kayaking, dolphin watches, parasailing, jet-ski, bike trails, mopeds, beaches and women-only cruises.

Key West boasts one of the only coral reefs in the continental United States. Whilst here the Sunset Celebration at Mallory Square is a must - you will see jugglers, sword swallowers, tightrope walkers and characters that will amuse and delight you.

New Dawn
Caribbean Retreat & Guesthouse
PO Box 1512
Vieques, Puerto Rico 00765
Tel: (787) 741 0495

Woman run. Mostly women clientele. Guesthouse has 6 private bedrooms with shared bath or shower rooms. Bunk house sleeps eight. Also camping. Guesthouse has lounge, garden, bar, TV room, washing machine, telephone, iron. Children welcome. Some access for disabled travellers. Smoking outside only. Dinner and packed lunches can be provided. Vegetarian diets catered for. Open throughout the year. In-season rates: Guesthouse bedrooms are £40.00 per room, plus $10 each additional person; Bunkhouse is $18.00 per person; Tent site is $10.00 per person. Discounts available. Brochure available.

Situated 3 miles from the beach, this peaceful woman operated, women friendly retreat and guesthouse has been established some 11 years.   The simply furnished family and double rooms have shared bath and shower facilities.

New Dawn is designed for women who like to go barefoot and who don't need all the comforts of home. Its relaxed and peaceful atmosphere brings people back. For those who want to be active, volleyball, massages, nature walks, horseshoes, exercise classes, croquet, horse and bicycle riding are just some of the activities offered at New Dawn. Some equipment can be hired on site. A 'must' is the fascinating evening Phosphorescent Bay Trip, to see micro-organisms glow in the dark!

There are spacious decks, with swings and hammocks galore, an open kitchen, a comprehensive library collection and a combination dining/meeting area. Windows have views overlooking the Caribbean Sea and beautiful tropical scenes.

New Dawn has a restaurant and, when available, home grown produce is used in food preparation. For guests with children, there are playpens, highchairs and a baby sitting service. There are ramps to the house for disabled travellers and wheelchair users, but access is not possible upstairs.

Over C's Guesthouse
940 Elysian Fields Avenue
New Orleans
Louisiana 70117
Tel: (504) 943 7166 or 945 9328

Women only guest house and Women's Club. Three bedroom suites with king size beds and private bath. The suites also have microwave, fridge, cable TV and telephone. Lounge, Piano room, Verandah, bar, iron. No children. No pets under most circumstances. Smoking permitted. Open throughout the year. Room rates start at $85.00 for double occupancy. Certain rates apply for Mardi Gras and Jazz Festivals. Brochure available.

Built around the turn of the century, this lovely old place is situated very close to the famous French Quarter. The owner, Charlene, is proud to have been an early civil rights participant, who opened New Orleans' oldest world-famous women's club (Charlene's) some 20 years ago. In 1990 she opened the Over C's Guesthouse and describes her establishment as political and very friendly.

Described as a "great getaway", guests are welcomed with complimentary champagne.

The French Quarter offers visitors the chance to enjoy its antique shops, excellent restaurants, museums, bars, discos and casinos. Also worth visiting is Jackson Square and St Louis Cathedral.

There are also special festivals and events during the year including jazz festivals and the famous Mardis Gras.

Bourgoyne Guest House
839 Bourbon Street
New Orleans
Louisiana 70116
Tel: (504) 525 3983 or 524 3621

Woman run guest house. Five bedrooms with private bath, kitchen and telephone. TV in some bedrooms. Children welcome. No pets. Garden, telephone, washing machine, iron. Smoking permitted everywhere. Open throughout the year. Room rates $70.00 to $160.00. Brochure available.

Established 20 years, this 1830's French/Spanish style townhouse is situated in the heart of the historic French quarter of New Orleans. The Bourgoyne has balconies, galleries, winding staircases and a hidden courtyard filled with exotic and subtropical plants where guests can retreat from the excitement and hullabaloo of Bourbon Street.

Guest accommodation ranges from cosy studios to spacious one and two-bedroom suites of unusual style and elegance. All rooms are furnished with antiques and all have private baths, kitchens, air conditioning and telephones.

The French Quarter offers visitors the chance to enjoy its antique shops, fine restaurants, museums, bars and discos.

Golden Gate Cottage

Golden Gate Cottage
RR7 Box 182
Eureka Springs
Arkansas 72631-9225
Tel: (501) 253 5291

**Women only. Three bedrooms with private bath and shower.
TV/VCR in bedroom, coffee-making facilities, fridge, radio,
telephone, iron. Hot tub, charcoal grill, ceiling fans, patio and
deck overlooking lake. No children. No pets. Smoking
permitted. Prices range from $40.00 to $55.00 per room per
night. Brochure available.**

Built in the 1980's, the cottage is ideally placed for guests to enjoy
the beauty of Tablerock Lake and the White River. It can
accommodate up six people in three double rooms which can be
made interconnecting if required. Each unit has its own separate
entrance and all have a private bath and shower.   There is a
furnished kitchenette.

From the bedrooms you can see the lake which is "just over the
road" and ideal for swimming. In front of the cottage is a nature
walking trail that has the river on one side and beautiful cliffs on
the other.

To ensure guests feel welcome your host provides complimentary
coffee, tea and hot chocolate and a range of books, games, and
movies. She also enjoys entertaining and has "spur of the moment"
get-togethers.

Nearby Beaver Lake consists of 483 miles of shoreline providing
walking trails, water sports, fishing and camping facilities. There
are also plenty of other things to do and see locally, including
visiting churches, museums, caves, art galleries, craft stores, and the
lakes. Part of everyone's itinerary should be the musical hoedown
shows and the outdoor opera (summer only).

Women's Holiday Retreat
318 Red Rock Road
Silver City, New Mexico
Mailing address: PO Box 330
Tyrone, New Mexico 88065, USA

Women only retreat with self-catering guesthouse, camping and RV site. Guesthouse has one twin bedroom and private bathroom. Garden. Children welcome. No pets. No smoking. Open all year. Rates $10.00 per woman, per night (in house), $5.00 per woman, per night in tent or RV. Brochure available.

This women's retreat is situated approximately 20 miles from Silver City, in the southwest of New Mexico. Nestling in the middle of the Burro Mountains, the retreat is set in 5 acres of land and offers wonderful scenic views as far as the eye can see. The area offers peace and tranquillity and a place to restore. There is a pond, campfire and barbecue.

There are deer, mule-deer, coyotes, hares, bobcats, lynx, raccoons, foxes and many colourful birds, including bluebirds, owls, hawks, falcons, turkeys and even the state bird of New Mexico, the roadrunner, breeding on the land around the Retreat.

The area enjoys mild summers and winters. In the summer there is often a cooling breeze which makes the temperature very bearable. The surrounding land consists of a stony, grass grown, soft rising hill with pinons, junipers, live oaks, cane-chollas and yuccas.

Silver City has a university, many good restaurants and cafes, and an excellent bookshop. The historic downtown area of Silver City has museums, art galleries and concerts. You can visit ghost towns, the 'catwalk', indian cliff dwellings, the 'City of Rocks', 'Rockhound State Park' and many more interesting places. There is also horse riding and skiing.

Your host is a 40 year old, born under the sign of Aries. She is a singer and astrologer, traveller, gambler and good cook. She has a good local knowledge and can direct you to the Land lesbian gathering that takes place in September each year.

The Triangle Inn, PO Box 3235
Santa Fe, New Mexico 87501
Tel: (505) 455 3375
E-mail: TriangleSF@aol.com
Homepage: http://www.newmexico.com/~triangle/

**Women run and mainly lesbian clientele. Eight double suites
and one family suite (casita) all with private bath and air
conditioning . TV/VCR and CD/stereo and hairdryer in each
room. Garden. Spa. Outdoor fireplace. Telephone, iron.
Children welcome. Large outside play area. Disabled travellers
can be accommodated - all rooms are ground floor with one
casita fully wheelchair accessible. Pets welcome (for small
charge). Smoking in some rooms. Vegetarians and vegans can
be catered for, plus some other special diets with advance notice.
Double occupancy rates range from $70.00 (Winter) and $90.00
(Summer). Open all year. Brochure available.**

Situated about 10 miles from downtown Santa Fe, at the foot of the
Sangre de Cristo mountains, this country inn bed and breakfast has
been established 10 years. The Inn's nine distinctive 'casitas'
(cottages) offer a variety of options for the visitor. Regardless of
which one you choose, special attention has been paid to the details
in each of the rooms.

All rooms have kitchenettes and complimentary gourmet coffee tea,
cocoa and snacks. There are luxury linens, bathrobes, spa towels
and bath slippers for your comfort and a TV/VCR and CD/stereo for
your enjoyment.   Five of the suites have private fireplaces. A
scrumptious expanded continental breakfast is provided for you, in
your casita, each day.

One casita, Piñon House, has two bedrooms, with authentic vigas,
hardwood floors and kiva fireplace and can accommodate up to six
people. It has a private courtyard, spacious kitchen, sunny dining
area, master bedroom with king size bed and a second bedroom with
a double bed - reached through an old pueblo style door. This casita
is non-smoking.

Continued overleaf...

The Inn has two large courtyards for guests to use. The Hacienda Courtyard has a stunning portal and outdoor fireplace, in a delightful setting where afternoon refreshments are provided.

The Main Courtyard, around which most of the casitas are situated, has extensive plantings, a large hot tub, a deck and sunbathing area.

Your Innkeepers, Karen and Sarah, have excellent local knowledge and will be able to advise you of various activities and trips. They retired from the "real" world so they could live in a gay-only environment - and they love it! They are both gourmet cooks and animal lovers.

Santa Fe is one of the most interesting and historical places to visit in the US South West. The down town area is known for its art galleries, art shops and great restaurants. The area is home to seven Native American tribes and the Inn is surrounded by their land. You can visit the living pueblos as well as the ruins of the Anasazi culture. Spaniards came through this area and left their imprint with guat churches and adobe missions. The area has a wealth of craft places to visit plus wonderful outdoor activities, such as hiking, skiing, snow shoeing, horseback riding, biking, gliding and balloon riding.

Hawk, I'm Your Sister
PO Box 9109
Santa Fe
New Mexico 87504-9109
Tel: (505) 984 2268

Women's Wilderness Canoe Trips. Canoes, paddles, life jackets, tents, cooking and eating utensils, toilet tissue are provided by Hawk. Guests provide sleeping bag and personal items. Cost of trip generally includes transportation from airport to departure point. Costs vary according to trip. Comprehensive brochure available.

Hawk, I'm Your Sister was founded by Beverley Antaeus and has guided river trips since 1975. She is highly qualified in her craft and has a great love for the outdoor habitat and its wildlife.

In a safe, supportive environment, without competition, women of all ages and degrees of experience are encourage to recognise and appreciate their own physical and inner strengths and abilities. Group members share daily tasks, including food preparation and clean-up, carrying and loading canoes and digging latrines.

The food is good and the team prepare generous, nutritious meals from the best ingredients, including bountiful fresh vegetables, fresh and dried fruits, whole grains, chicken and fish. Vegetarian and other special diets can be accommodated when requested in advance. The aromatic creations from the Dutch ovens are delightful alternatives to the dreary, dried food diet we used to expect on camping trips.

Some examples of trips: Missouri River, Montana. A 7-day, 46 mile trip. A Writing Retreat which has aims to bring forth forms of poetry from the inspiration of the landscape and from within.

Small Hope Bay, Andros Island, Bahamas. A 9-day holiday learning to snorkel, sail, wind surf and scuba. Daily snorkelling excursions are made from the shore and to the reef, with opportunities to try scuba diving. Experienced divers will be enthralled with the wrecks and walls and blue holes of the reef.

Paradise Ranch
135 Kachina Drive
Sedona
Arizona 86336
Tel: (520) 282 9769

Women only guesthouse. Self-contained accommodation with one bedroom with private bath, kitchen and sitting area. TV/VCR, swimming pool, washing machine, telephone, iron. Hot tub, charcoal grill, ceiling fans No children. No pets. No smoking inside. Teepee on property. Open throughout the year. Rates: $85.00 for 1 woman per night, $95.00 for 2 women per night. Brochure available.

Established 8 years, this women operated rustic, private guesthouse, set amongst fruit trees and mature pine and juniper trees, is a quiet place to relax away from your usual routine. There is an outdoor stone BBQ, outdoor tables, chairs and a hammock and swing bench.

Paradise Ranch is described as a place of vision and healing and is dedicated to bringing about a balance of energy on the Earth and to the Earth Mother. It is located in the enchanting Red Rocks of Sedona, said by some to be one of the most beautiful and spiritual places on earth, and is an area that contains many energy vortices. The owners work together to help bring people's dreams into reality, combining spiritual principles with practical applications.

Included in the varied programmes and services, Paradise Ranch offers crystal healing and aura cleansing, star chamber experiences, massage and facials, transformation therapy, bonding ceremonies and mediations. Guests can also purchase crystals, jewellery, tapes, cards, posters, books and art objects.

Locally you can swim, fish, go horseback riding, and hiking. In Sedona there are good restaurants and a variety of galleries and shops.

Mom's Bed and Breakfast
5903 West Cortez
Glendale
Arizona 85304
Tel: (602) 979 2869

Women only guesthouse. Three en-suite bedrooms. Lounge, garden, TV room, washing machine, telephone, iron, hairdryers. Fireplace. Tea and coffee making facilities. Large swimming pool. Sun deck. Hot tub. BBQ grills. Thomas Organ. Pool table. No children. No pets. Smoking on comfortable patio area only. Can accommodate disabled travellers -- some wheelchair access and all rooms on ground level. Lunch, dinner and packed lunches can be provided. Snacks on arrival. Special diets can be catered for with advance notice. Open throughout year. Summer rates start at $75.00 for a double occupancy and $85.00 in High Season. Brochure.

Situated in an area known as the Valley of the Sun, Mom's wants to offer guests a real home from home. Operated by Betty, whose daughter is a lesbian and of whom she is clearly very proud, Mom's offers privacy and a positive welcome.

There are three double bedrooms but these can be used differently, according to the number of guests and size of party. Additional guests can be accommodated with sleeping bags. When available, fresh cut flowers, from the breathtaking garden, are placed in guests' rooms to welcome them.

One of the rooms (The Green Room) opens to an indoor Arcadia garden room and has its own exit to the pool - wonderful if you wish to swim by moonlight and then make your way back to the 9ft circular bed, or take a bath in the sunken 'tub for two'.

For those wanting even more privacy, a separate Guest House with a full kitchen is available for rent, which has its own pool table. . Betty provides an excellent expanded continental, or full catered breakfast for her guests.

Continued overleaf...

140

Mom's Bed and Breakfast continued

When available, fresh vegetable garden produce is used in meal preparation and, if guests would like to request a candlelit dinner, Betty would be very pleased to take orders.

In the lounge is a gas-fired fireplace, with its sunken 'conversation pit' and in the intriguing navigational chart room you can relax in front of a big screen TV. Mom's has its own large swimming pool with a private pool area set in large gardens of mature olive and palm trees.

There's plenty of tea and coffee available and a library/reading room with a choice of books, maps and papers. When you are ready to explore, Betty will be only too pleased to assist you with her knowledge of local activities and attractions. Mom's is planning some courses and there is also a local Women's Centre that has many activities planned.

Commitment Ceremonies or other celebrations can be arranged.

Montecito House
PO Box 42352
Tucson
Arizona 85733
Tel: (520) 327 8586 or 795 7592

Woman run. Two double bedrooms, one with private bath and one with shared bath. Lounge, TV room, telephone, iron, washing machine. Pinball machine. Air-conditioning. Caravan. Smoking on outside on covered porch only. Self-catering breakfast, with vegetarians catered for with advance notice. Children may be accommodated - please discuss in advance. No pets. Summer rates from $35.00 double occupancy, Winter rates from $40.00 double occupancy. Reservations recommended, particularly in February.

Tucson is situated in southern Arizona, with easy access from Phoenix and only 1½ hours from Mexico.

Montecito House has been established 9 years, offering comfortable beds and a good welcome. Guests make their own breakfast, with home grown produce when in season, which can then be washed down with freshly squeezed juice from the Grapefruit tree in the garden. The house is within walking distance of tennis courts, pool, Jacuzzi, library, professional baseball, two golf courses and a zoo.

Fran has lived in the area for 12 years and has considerable local knowledge which she will happily share with you to help you plan your trips and activities. She regards her B&B as a hobby rather than a business and particularly enjoys meeting people from around the world.

Tucson is a destination resort town with lots to see and do. Day trips can easily be arranged to mining towns, Tombstone, Mexico, State and National parks, Spanish missions, artists colonies, Indian reservations, desert or mountain habitats, museums and much more! The area is popular for hiking and mountain biking.

The Mango House
2087 Iholena Street
Honolulu, Hawaii 96817
Tel/fax: (808) 595 6682
E-mail: mango@pixi.com

Women run bed and breakfast. Two double bedrooms and one family bedroom. Two bedrooms have private bathroom (jacuzzi tub) and one is shared. Hairdryer in room. Lounge, TV room, garden, telephone, washing machine, iron. Children of 10 years and older welcome at the Inn. No pets. Smoking outside only. The self-catering Mango Cottage sleeps 2-4 people, has a TV, telephone and fully equipped kitchen. Ceiling fans and air conditioning in living room. No smoking in cottage. Children of any age welcome in cottage.
Inn and Cottage open throughout the year. Inn rates $63.00 - $93.00 per room per night for double occupancy. Cottage rates from $89.00 double occupancy. Discount for longer stays. Brochure available.

Situated on a mountainside, The Mango House has stunning panoramic view of Honolulu, Punchbowl Crater, the harbour and the Pacific Ocean. Catering primarily to our "rainbow family", Tracy and Marga run a beautiful and healing establishment where guests wake to wonderful bird calls and views of mango trees and a lychee tree. Their delicious continental breakfast includes coffee, homemade breads and mango jam, fresh island fruits and juice.

The Mango Cottage is fully furnished with a queen bed and sleeper sofa. Bedding, beach and bath towels are provided and there is a free washer-dryer on the premises. The cottage is fully carpeted and up one flight of stairs. The living room and bedroom overlook a park, Honolulu city lights and the ocean. Both the Mango House and the cottage are 15 minutes drive from Waikiki and a scenic 20 minute drive to Kailua, a famous windsurfing mecca.

Your Innkeepers are very friendly and helpful, offering advice on the best restaurants, local events run for the rainbow community, and anything else you need to know to help you enjoy your holiday. Both women scuba dive and allow guests to borrow snorkelling gear, beach chairs, towels, ice and even the cooler!

Alison Reitz
Cloud Canyon Backpacking
PO Box 41359, Santa Barbara
California 93140
E-mail: areitz@silcom.com

Wilderness trips for women and international expeditions. Small groups (usually 6-8 people). Non smoking. Fee includes all meals on the trail. Special diets can be catered for. Rates for a 7-9 day wilderness backpack trip in Utah start from $700.00. An 11-day Alaska trip starts from $1200.00. Price does not include transportation to meeting place. Brochure available.

Alison has been leading trips in the outdoors for 7 years. She has a Masters degree in Geology and is a writer and photographer. Alison continues to enjoy and wonder at the way in which time spent in the wilderness can change people's lives. Experience the freedom and confidence that living only with the essentials and helping each other can bring. Every wilderness trip is an adventure.

Cloud Canyon Backpacking provides all food and cooking utensils, with group members bringing their own personal gear and camping equipment. All expeditions include short classes in all aspects of wilderness travel, use of equipment, food preparation, safety, route finding, good judgment and others. Beginners welcome!

The Utah trips, usually in May, June, September and October, are in an area of the USA's spectacular desert canyon country, with beautiful rock outcroppings and rushing streams. The Alaska trip, usually in August, includes ferry ride, glacier viewing and visits to historic mining towns.

New for 1998 is a two-part trip to the South Island of New Zealand. Go backpacking in the mountains, along the coast and in the fjord lands of the south. Learn about the Maori culture and New Zealand natural history and go white water rafting, cave rafting and biking.

Bellflower
PO Box 867
Mendocino
California 95460
Tel: (707) 937 0783

**Women only cabin.   Self catering accommodation with one
double room, living room, private deck with small water
fountain. Hot tub. Fully equipped kitchen with fridge, stove,
toaster oven and coffee maker. Garden. No pets. Smoking
outside only. Open throughout the year. Rates are $65.00 per
night, with a 2-night minimum stay. Discount for longer stays.
No brochure.**

Bellflower was built by women and is set on 10 acres of land and
surrounded by like-minded women neighbours.   It is located on the
Mendocino Coast, which is noted for its beaches, crafts, hiking and
biking trails, riding and kayaking.   There many shops and
restaurants and a thriving women's community.

The large cabin has a wood burning stove for your comfort. There
is also a large hot tub. The owner is a landscape designer and plant
collector and arranges interesting garden tours May to August.

Women in Motion
PO Box 4533
Oceanside
California 9205-4533
Tel: (619) 754 6747

**Activity holidays and tours for women. Offices closed at
Thanksgiving and Christmas. Rates vary according to trip.
Detailed brochure available.**

The Women in Motion offices are located in Oceanside and offer
vacation packages, cruises, tours and adventure for women
travellers.   Their extensive brochure details the various holidays
and activities on offer and you can now register your trip, or get
details of updates, via the Internet on http://GoWomen.com.

Your tour partners personally survey each site and test out the
various activities to ensure their suitability for participants. Your
trip leaders and instructors are all highly qualified in their specialist
areas.

Children can be accommodated in most circumstances when
accompanied by their legal guardian - please check when making
initial enquiries.   Provision can be made for disabled travellers but
this varies from trip to trip. Pets can be accepted at some resorts.
Food or meals are provided with some holidays and vegetarians can
be catered for.

Examples of some of the variety of holidays and activities are:

A 5-day New Mexico vacation and tour in Santa Fe, starts and ends
at the luxurious El Dorado Hotel, in the midst of the area's artist
community. A varied and interesting trip where you can experience
world-class opera, true hospitality and fine dining. There will be
opportunities for sight-seeing, llama trekking, white-water rafting,
golf and shopping!

Continued overleaf...

Women in Motion continued

A Nordic Adventure cross-country Skiing Weekend in Yosemite Valley. Based at an elegant mountain retreat, you have a choice of skis or snowshoes. Muscles are soothed in the evening with hot toddies and a hot tub!

The Woman Craft vacation planned for February 1998, in Tucson, Arizona - the perfect time of year to be in Arizona. You will stay in a renovated 'Wild West' hotel and will learn about Indian culture, arts and history. The trip was inspired by women artists and offers lessons in tile making, painting, drawing and sculpture.

Perhaps you should also consider what you might like to be doing on New Year's Eve 1999? If you want to spend it amongst friends, how about heading for Hawaii on a trip planned to run from 26th December 1999 to January 2nd 2000.

Other vacations are designed for golf enthusiasts, women who enjoy biking, rock climbing, canoeing, wine-tasting and most other activities you can think of! You might like to travel on the Temptress Voyager to Belize/Guatamala. The brochure describes all!

Adventure Women
PO Box 1408
Santa Cruz
California 95061
Tel: (408) 479 0473

Women only accommodation and activity charter tours. Four double and six single rooms, all with private bath. Children welcome. Wheelchair access and fragrance-free environment. No pets. TV room, telephone. Swimming pool. No smoking. Lunch, dinner and snacks available. All special diets can be catered for - please advise in advance. Open throughout the year. Rates for accommodation and sailing trip are $1,200.00 per person. Brochure available.

Betty has run Adventure Women for 5 years and offers accommodation and charters by ecology conscious operators who actively promote care of the marine environment. She is an artist, photographer and eco-psychologist who arranges tours for women. Group size is limited to ensure a personal experience for all participants. All tours are smoke, alcohol, drug and scent free for those with chemical sensitivities.

This historic bed and breakfast accommodation in Key West has comfortable rooms, with kitchen facilities. Breakfast and any other meals are eaten in a communal room where guests can each enjoy the company of the other. Food is freshly prepared, using home-grown produce when available.

Betty arranges dolphin tours where you can swim, snorkel or sail/kayak with dolphins - try her Kona Coast Eco-Scape tour offers 6-nights in a deluxe Oceanfront Condominium, whale and dolphin watch activities, snorkeling and coral reef ecology, kayaking and shore exploration. There is also free time for guests to explore the area at their own pace.

Locally, visitors can enjoy the attractions of the Bay Key West, the Florida Keys and the Marine Underwater State Park Preserve.

Country Comfort B&B
5104E Valencia Drive
Orange 92669, California.
Tel: (714) 532 2802

> **Women only bed and breakfast. Two bedrooms with private bath. Lounge, TV room, bar, telephone, iron, washing machine. Garden. Swimming pool. Jacuzzi. Fireplace fires. Wall library. Well-supervised children welcome. No pets. Disabled accessible with adaptive equipment. Smoking outside only. Snacks can be provided. Vegetarian, diabetic, low-fat, vegan diets can be provided. Rates $65.00 per room per night, single or double occupancy (sorry no credit cards). Brochure available.**

Located in a quiet residential area, Geri and Joanne welcome guests with a country-style hospitality which includes a delicious breakfast, including scotch eggs, stuffed french toast, fruits and assorted beverages. Vegetarian selections are also available.

The bedrooms have private bathrooms, cable TV, ceiling fan, fridge and hairdryer. The 'Turn of the Century' room opens onto the atrium, with a private entrance and pleasant sitting area. It is furnished with a King-size featherbed and antique chifferobe. The 'Library Room' delights book lovers and has two single beds which can be made up into one double bed.

In the family room is a laser disc and a large 60" TV and VCR. Also available is a fax and photocopier. Guests can use the fitness equipment, swim in the pool, or simply relax in the jacuzzi. There is a bar, which provides complimentary evening refreshments.

Geri is a management consultant and executive coach and has a keen interest in information technology. Joanne is a social worker with a flair for cooking and a love of books.

Orange is a lovely city, 40 minutes from Los Angeles' theatre district, airport and museums. Much nearer is Disneyland, Anaheim Convention Centre, Knotts Berry Farm, the beach and Angel Stadium. The local repertory theatre and performing arts centre can compete with New York and Los Angeles in their offerings. At nearby Long Beach visit the Queen Mary.

Bock's Bed & Breakfast
1448 Willard Street
San Francisco
California 94117
Tel: (415) 664 6842
Fax: (415) 664 1109

Women only.   Three units, each with private or semi-private bath, private telephone, TV and coffee and tea service. Also available: fridge, microwave, iron, washing machine, hairdryer and fax machine. Expanded continental breakfast. Special diets catered for with advance notice. No smoking indoors.   Rates start at $40.00 for single occupancy and $60.00 for double occupancy with two nights minimum stay. Discount for longer stays. Brochure available.

This restored Edwardian residence has offered a casual and comfortable hospitality to guests from around the world since 1980. It is situated in Parnassus Heights, a lovely residential neighbourhood which has a multitude of shops, cafes and good restaurants. There is excellent public transport nearby, providing easy access to every part of the city.

The house still has its original virgin redwood panelling in the dining room and foyer, exposed mahogany and inlaid oak floors and the original redwood and oak staircase. Your host is a native San Franciscan and can help visitors enjoy all the best that the area can offer and can take you on a city tour if required. She provides a delicious continental breakfast, including fresh juice, fresh fruit, granola and a variety of different baked goods every day, including home-baked bread.

The 'Mary Ellen' unit has a private bath, private deck for sunbathing, a dramatic view of the city and one Queen and one twin sofa bed. All bedrooms have hand-made quilts and two rooms have lovely city views.

The last week of June is Gay Pride Week, an especially festive time at Bock's and throughout San Francisco. The house is situated just 20 minutes from the Castro district, famous for its gay community.

Shakti Cove Cottages
PO Box 385
Ocean Park, Washington 98640
Tel: (360) 665 4000

Women run. Ten cottages - three with double bedrooms, six with single bedrooms and one with a twin bedroom. Each cottage has: Sitting area and fully equipped kitchen. Shower room. Cable TV. Garden. Outside there is a BBQ grill and hammock. Pond. Linens provided. Smoking permitted. Children can be accommodated if supervised by parents. Rates: $70.00 per cottage, per night. Winter special: 3 weeks for price of 2 (excluding USA holidays). Brochure available.

Built in 1939, these recently renovated cabins have sheltered many generations of clam diggers and beachcombers. They are located on the beautiful Long Beach Peninsula at the very southwest corner of Washington State. It's the kind of retreat where you can drive onto the property and "your whole soul is immediately refreshed"!

There are ten separate cabins, all of which are very clean and rustic, set in a semi-circle and nestled in a grove of trees. A 5 minute walk over a footpath takes you to the Pacific Ocean - just follow the sound of the surf.. The cabins are on 3 secluded acres of lush green woodland, bordered by a mill stream that looks as calm as a pond. Guests can enjoy the various birds that visit the lake, especially the great blue heron that 'hangs out' there.

Liz and Celia have been running Shakti Cove Cottages for 8 years and, whilst the cottages are not always women only (all 'couples' are welcome), your hosts are committed to providing a safe place for women to retreat.

The Long Beach Peninsula hosts many festivals throughout the year, including the Garlic Festival, Cranberry and Water Music Festival and the International Kite Festival, to name but a few! There are 28 miles of sandy beaches and nearby are the world famous Oyster Beds. You can visit the lighthouses at Cape Disappointment and North Head in Fort Canby State Park, or the wildlife refuge at the north end of the peninsular, ride the go-carts and eat taffy in Long Beach, or just stay at Shakti Cove and relax.

Fish Creek Lodging
Warm River
PO Box 833, Ashton
Idaho 83420
Tel: (208) 652 7566

**Women only self-catering log cabin. Three double beds, with
private bathroom. Lounge, TV/VCR room, telephone, iron.
Fully equipped kitchen. No children. Pets with prior approval.
No smoking in cabin. Rates are $80.00 per night for double
occupancy, plus $15.00 for each additional person. Two nights
minimum stay. Weekly rate is $400.00 for double occupancy.
Monthly rates available. Brochure available.**

Hand-built by women, the log cabin is fully equipped and enjoys the
most beautiful views of mountains, meadows. In a secluded
position, the cabin is surrounded by thousands of acres of national
forest.

Your private log cabin is furnished with all you need to relax and
enjoy yourself. Meals can be easily prepared in the fully equipped
kitchen and then eaten on your own private deck - but don't be
surprised if you are joined by a neighbouring fox or moose! In the
evening you can warm yourself by the wood stove and be lulled to
sleep by the sound of gentle breezes whispering through the aspens
and the quiet call of coyotes.

Within easy reach is the world famous Yellowstone National Park,
where you can visit 'Old Faithful' and gaze at the peaceful herds of
elk and bison; Jackson Hole, Wyoming, and Teton National Park.
These areas offer you unique shops, informative museums and
galleries.

Whether you enjoy hiking, world-class fly fishing, skiing, viewing
wildlife, or just relaxing, Fish Creek Lodging offers the opportunity
for you to enjoy them all. Your host lives in the area and has the
advantage of excellent local knowledge. She runs horseback riding
events, including trail riding in the Teton Mountain Range.

Bar H Ranch
Idaho
Tel: (208) 354 2906
or 1-800 247 1444 (in USA)

Women only ranch. Two double bedrooms with private bathroom. Lounge, dining area, telephone, iron. TV and stereo. Fully equipped kitchen with dishwasher, oven etc. Deck. BBQ. No children. Pets with prior approval. Teepee. Loft $580.00 per week for double occupancy. Trail riding $100.00 per day (all equipment provided). Brochure available.

Situated in the Teton Valley and nestled between the Teton and Big Hole Mountain ranges, the Bar H ranch enjoys sweeping pasture views, aspens and willow and, of course, horses and cattle. The owner is a third generation cattle rancher and the only woman in the area operating a ranch with female assistants.

This is a vacation for people who want to experience life on an authentic working cattle ranch. You can either join in with ranch life or choose a less structured and more restful vacation. For those who join in, the weeks activities are a combination of daily ranch work and personal free time. If you so choose, you can saddle your own horse, move cattle and fix fences.

During your free time you can relax, hike, canoe, cycle, fish or go sightseeing. Nearby is the Yellowstone National Park, Grand Teton National Park and Jackson Hole. Trail riding in the high country will enable you to experience its majestic peaks and glacial lakes.

At the end of the day relax in the old-fashioned, claw foot bath tub and warm yourself by the wood stove. Alternatively, experience the serenity of a night in an authentic 18 foot Sioux teepee and sense the peace and power celebrated by the Sioux for hundreds of years.

North Crow Ranch
2360 North Crow Road
Ronan, Montana 59864
Tel: (406) 676 5169

Women only ranch and campsite. One furnished cabin with wood stove. Covered patio. Four teepees. One shared shower room. Three outhouses (with solar showers). Garden and lawn with picnic tables. Children welcome. Pets welcome on a leash. Smoking in designated areas. Rates: Camping $10.00 p/p per night, Teepee $15.00 p/p per night, Cabin $20.00 p/p per night. For group rates of 7 or more people, take 10% of above prices. Open May 15th to October 15th. Brochure available.

The ranch and campsite resort is set in 40 acres and combines a tasteful balance of comfort and outdoor activity in a natural setting of forest, field and stream. For your enjoyment the ranch has two communal fire pits, a hot tub, volleyball and badminton areas, basketball and horseshoe pits - and a creek! Outdoor speakers are wired for music and Saturday night dances.

Your host has been running the ranch as a gay guest business for the past 16 years and is a native Montanan with extensive guide and fly fishing skills. If pre-arranged, she is very willing to taken women into the wilderness areas to explore or fish in the streams.

Breakfast and dinner are served hot and plentiful daily. Some home grown produce is used, including carrots, tomatoes, cilantro, basil and dill. The cabin is comfortable and clean and the teepees have carpeting and a fire pit - a different way to sleep under the stars! For campers the outdoor solar showers are always hot and the privies are clean and convenient.

Locally there is an annual Labour Day all women's event. Close by in the Mission Mountains there are wilderness trials for hiking and the mountain lakes and streams provide great fishing. Within 15 minutes drive is the largest freshwater lake in the west, where you can go swimming, boating, sailing and windsurfing. There are also opportunities to play golf. At Flathead Valley you can try river raft floats, visit rodeos, the buffalo range, museums and the summer theatre. There's even an Indian Pow Wow!

Australia and New Zealand

Witchencroft
PO Box 685, Atherton 4883
Queensland, Australia
Tel: Jenny (070) 912 683
E:mail jj@bushnet.qld.edu.au

**Women only. Two self contained units each with double room,
fully furnished kitchen, TV and en suite bathroom facilities.
Washing machine, iron and telephone. Garden. All meals
available on request. No meat served. Special diets catered for -
please advise. Smoking outside only. Open throughout the year.
Rates: Single (with work exchange) from $15.00, and Double
from $32.00. Other rates: Single $50.00 and double $70.00.
Discounts for longer stays. Brochure available.**

Witchencroft is a landscaped , 5 acre organic farm, nestled in a
forest valley on the Atherton Tablelands, a tropical paradise of
lakes, waterfalls, country markets and local horse riding. The
Tablelands are 2,500 feet in altitude, are called the 'cool tropics' as
you escape the heat, humidity and biting insects of the coast. It is
uniquely placed to offer remarkably different ecosystems and
microclimates, within half an hour of Witchencroft. It is Australia's
oldest and perhaps most well-known women's guesthouse.

Only one hour's drive from Cairns, Witchencroft is an ideal base to
explore the coast and its hinterland, the Great Barrier Reef and
World Heritage tropical rainforest and dry Gulf Savannah.

Jenny has been operating the guesthouse since 1987. There are two
units, named *Hazel* and *Frances*, after Jenny's grandmothers. They
are attached to the main house by a verandah. Each self-contained
unit is very comfortably furnished and overlooks bush gardens. For
women on low income some form of work exchange is usually
available and this is then reflected in the price charged for
accommodation (see above for rates).

If you take a walk outside you will be in the company of free range
sheep, ducks, chickens and kelpies. The units are in a private
garden setting, have a private verandah in the middle of nature.

Continued overleaf ...

Delicious vegetarian meals are available on request and home grown produce, including organic fruits, vegetables, nuts and herbs, is used in food preparation wherever possible.

Guests can enjoy Witchencroft and relax around the bilabong and share the excitement of their day, whilst planning the next adventure! Jenny organises day walks, longer backpacking tours (2-6 nights) and 4WD adventures (up to 6 people) which involves 3-14 nights camping in generously varied sea and landscapes. All accommodation and tours are run on principles of minimal impact on the environment. Such is the diversity of the local landscape, fine weather can be virtually guaranteed all year round.

Trips are totally customised for guests, according to the weather. Just let Jenny know how much time you want to spend driving, walking, talking, swimming, relaxing and eating - and what your interests are - and she will come up with just the right itinerary. Swim in crystal clear waters, rivers and lakes, explore old Aboriginal tracks in pristine World Heritage Rainforests; discover the spectacular 'dry country' that few know about. Experience the wonder of this part of Australia with a guide who is in love with it!

Jenny is a physiotherapist in her early 40's and a 4th generation North Queenslander. She is a carer of injured and orphaned wildlife, especially flying foxes and is actively involved in a local bat rescue programme from October to March each year.

Orphan bats are fostered out with human parents for about 5 months and then gradually re-introduced into the wild. Anyone wanting to help in the rescue programme is welcome to visit the guesthouse in November and December each year. At any time Jenny is happy to share the fascinating and moving tales about her experiences fostering her baby bats! Jenny also has an interest in native plants and landscaping and has planted over 6,000 trees at Witchencroft.

Whilst in Scotland in 1986 Jenny came up with the name 'Witchencroft'. A croft is a small land holding where the crofter works the land but has outside work as well. Witchen is a common name for the Rowan tree, commonly beside the old stone cottages to keep away the bad witches.

A Slice of Heaven
Lot 3 (6916)
Pacific Highway,   Stokers Siding
New South Wales 2484, Australia
Tel: (066) 77 9276 or
(Mobile) 015 590 299
Contact: Fae or Carly

**Women only farm guesthouse. Two guestrooms in the main
house. Two separate studios. Double and single accommodation
available. Rooms have tea and coffee making facilities, fridge,
TV, cooker and microwave. TV room. Log fire. Washing
machine and iron available. Garden. Swimming pool.
Lunch, dinner, snacks and packed lunches can be provided. All
diets catered for. Smoking outside only. Open throughout the
year. Rates: $80.00 for doubles or $60.00 for single per night,
including breakfast. Brochure available.**

Appropriately called 'A Slice of Heaven', this 20 year old brick and
tile built Australian home, set in 12 acres, offers women a
wonderful opportunity to enjoy a rural retreat amongst friends and
like-minded women. Fae and Carly treat guests as they wish to be
treated when on holiday - and they expect to be treated exceptionally
well! Everything you could want is provided at A Slice of Heaven
and nothing is too much trouble.

Set in a rainforest environment created by the two women, using
permaculture principles, this retreat offers cosy and comfortable
accommodation in a relaxed, friendly and welcoming atmosphere.
There are the two guest rooms in the main house, a self-contained
studio in the newly appointed Barn near the tropical orchard and
tennis court and another separate studio beside the saltwater pool
and summerhouse.   There are lovely views of the tropical garden
and pool and to welcome guests, there are flowers in the bedrooms.

Breakfast is generally served in the Cabana, alongside the bilabong-
style saltwater pool. You will find that breakfast is nutritious, more
than ample and will set you up for the day! Fae, a gourmet cook,
uses home grown produce, including vegetables and tropical fruits.

Continued overleaf ...

159

A Slice of Heaven continued

If you would like to eat at the retreat, Fae can serve a variety of delicious meals on request. Alternatively, there are facilities for self-catering or a choice of charming restaurants and cafes locally. As well as the perfect base for exploring the Northern Rivers area and tourist belt of North South Wales, the retreat can be enjoyed simply for itself. It has plenty of facilities to keep you happily occupied: a saltwater swimming pool and spa; mini gym; tennis court; pool table; recreational dam; bush walking tracks right on the property; library/video library; outdoor BBQ's and a huge bath tub!

There are various optional workshops and events running during the year at A Slice of Heaven, including International Cooking, Permaculture, Craft Activities, Liver Cleansing Diet Courses and Growing Old Disgracefully! Other special events guests can enjoy at and around the retreat are the celebration of Christmas Day in July, a Women Only Fair and Market Day, a Women Only Sports Day and the monthly dinner parties catering for up to 24 people.

For many years now, Fae and Carly have been busy planting trees, improving the home and making additions to the farm. If you explore the retreat you will find that the two women have planted some 4,000 trees, including many rainforest trees, native shrubs and tropical fruit trees. Seventy percent of their property is natural sub-tropical rainforest and their efforts have enhanced the natural beauty of their small farm.

Within a ½ hour radius of A Slice of Heaven are pristine beaches, Coolagatta Gold Coast and Byron Bay, mountain climbing at Mount Warning, where the sun first lights Australia, rainforest national parks, country craft markets, pottery and art galleries, quaint villages, large country towns and beach townships. Brisbane is but a two hour drive. Head north, and within a short drive, you will come to Murwillumbah, Mulumbiby and Nimbin - make sure you take a day trip to this uniquely amazing town.

Generous discounts are offered for groups of six or more for stays of seven nights or more. Details available on request. All in all, given the accommodation, the setting, the situation and the welcome, this clearly isn't called A Slice of Heaven for nothing!
(Please note: From the UK direct dial is 0061 66 779 276)

Waiheke Women's Guesthouse
12 Te Aroha Avenue, Hekerua Bay
Waiheke Island, Auckland, New Zealand
Tel: (NZ 09) 372 9284

Women only. Villa. Four double bedrooms. Shared bathroom. Sitting room. Garden. Washing machine, iron and telephone. Children welcome. No pets. Smoking outside only. Rates: $20.00 per woman per night. Linen, bedding and towels provided. Open throughout the year. Brochure available.

The women's guesthouse is on Waiheke Island, by the city of Auckland. Described as a 'villa', it has been established 3 years and is situated 20 metres from the beach, in a very pretty setting surrounded by mature native bush. The area is ideal for bush walks. Outside is a fire and a bath!

The bedrooms are comfortably furnished and have balconies, with lovely scenic views. Guests share the kitchen facilities in the main house and use it to prepare meals and drinks.

Guests are welcome to borrow the dinghy and kayak during their stay to fully enjoy the nearby secluded bay. In the villa guests are welcome to browse through the books and play music on the facilities provided. The owner is a potter with a studio on the property. She will be pleased to show you her work and can also help you with details of all that is going on locally.

Waiheke Island is a popular holiday location with lovely beaches, good art galleries, cafes and a weekly market - all of which are within walking distance of the villa.

The Mermaid
1 Epuni Street
Wellington, New Zealand
Tel/Fax: 04 384 4511
E-mail: mermaid@sans.vuw.ac.nz

Women only guesthouse. Four double rooms. One en suite (Latino Room), one shared bathroom, plus separate toilet. TV in most rooms. Guest lounge. Fully equipped kitchen. Off street parking. Children welcome. Open all year. Rates according to room taken: $68.00 to $120.00 per room, per night - all inclusive of breakfast. Smoking permitted on the deck. Brochure available.

The Mermaid is a turn of the century building and all of the older features, such as stairway, architraves and windows have been restored. The guesthouse offers a safe, comfortable environment and has an atmosphere where women feel at ease.

Much attention has been to the comfort and enjoyment of guests. There are robes, large towels, fragrant soaps and hairdryers in all bedrooms. In the lounge a pool table, CD and tape system and large range of magazines and books are all available to enhance your stay. Guests are given a glass of complimentary wine on arrival and tea and fresh ground coffee is freely available at all times. Breakfast consists of a combination of bread, croissants, homemade jam, fresh fruits, cereals, cheese and juice.

The kitchen has all the facilities required for creating meals. The doors from the kitchen lead on to a deck, complete with hammock, that is partially enclosed and shaded by trees, but situated to catch the morning and evening sun in the summer months.

The bedrooms are individually decorated in a distinct colour and style of furnishing, using the skills of an award winning New Zealand designer. The high standard makes them a delight to be in.

It is just a 10 minute walk to the town centre and waterfront where visitors will find restaurants, cafes, theatres, the university and shopping. Your host provides extensive up to date networking information on women's accommodation and activities available.

Four Seasons Homestay
9 Mole Street, Greytown, Wairarapa
New Zealand
Tel: (06) 304 8454 - Alison and Pam

Women only bed and breakfast. Three bedroom. Two double and two could be used as a twin room. One en suite and one shared bathroom. Tea and coffee making facilities. Electric blankets and ceiling fans. Sitting room. TV. Washing machine, iron and telephone available. Garden. No children. No pets. Smoking outdoors - chairs provided undercover. Dinner and snacks by arrangement. Vegetarians catered for and other special diets with notice. Open throughout the year. B&B Rates: $55.00 per room for single occupancy, $85.00 - $95.00 per room for double occupancy. Brochure available.

The Four Seasons Homestay is a spacious home, that is quiet, sunny and welcoming. It is set in ½ acre of private, well established garden that is visited by many native birds. Located one hour from Wellington, the capital city of New Zealand, and a mere ten minutes from the interesting vineyard area of Martinborough, the B&B is run by two mature, professional women.

You will be greeted each morning by a full, cooked breakfast. For cooler days there is underfloor heating. Guests who are musical can enjoy the piano - and perhaps even entertain the other guests. To help you enjoy your stay the women are happy to provide candlelit dinners by arrangement. Fresh vegetables and herbs are used and you will immediately feel hungry with the delicious smells of your hosts' home baking.

One of the bedrooms has a balcony. All bedrooms have wonderful mountain views and, to help you feel welcomed, your host will put freshly cut flowers in the room as well as some nibbles. Guests are welcome to use the garden and a BBQ area is available.

You can spend your time alternating between relaxing and unwinding at the Homestay and discovering the special character of Greytown and the Wairarapa: gardens, fishing, tramping (back packing through mountains), canoeing, golf, arts and crafts, wineries and restaurants and much, much more.

Tanglewood
Queen Charlotte Drive, The Grove
Picton, RD. 1, New Zealand
Tel: 64-3-574 2080 (booking essential)

**Women only B&B. One double, one twin/double bedroom.
Both bedrooms en suite. Sitting room with TV. Kitchen area
and fridge. Tea and coffee making facilities. Balcony. Iron.
Electric blanket. Lunch, dinner, snacks and packed lunches
available by arrangement. Special diets catered for by prior
arrangement. No children. No pets. No smoking in main house.
Open most of the year. Rates: $80.00 per double/twin room and
$55.00 for a single room. Brochure available.**

Tanglewood is set in the Marlborough Sounds on the South Island,
in a road with wonderful scenic views. The new private, guest wing
is decorated to a high standard. The aim of the two women who run
Tanglewood is to provide quality accommodation for women which
offers privacy and every comfort in tranquil and idyllic
surroundings. Relax, or explore this beautiful area at your leisure.

This is a premier area, unsurpassed in natural beauty. An excellent
walking track is 10 minutes drive from the house and nearby are
wine trails, art and craft trails, fishing, swimming and other outdoor
activities. A choice of specific adventure pursuits are offered by
companies locally. The Inter-Island ferry is a 25 minute drive.

A full, three course breakfast is included in the tariff and all
cooking, except for bacon and eggs, is low cholesterol. Organically
grown home produce is used as much as possible in all meals.
Candlelit dinners are available, which you may have served in the
guests' quarters or in the main house, in the company of your hosts.

The bedrooms enjoy wonderful views and are comfortably
furnished. To help guests make the most of their stay, a selection
of books, maps and information about the area are provided.

Both women are widely travelled. Judy is from Yorkshire and
Denny is a native New Zealander. Both lived in the UK for many
years prior to settling in N.Z. Both are keen gardeners, keen
fisherwomen, cooks and avid readers.

Bushline Lodge
PO Box 28010, Christchurch 2
New Zealand
Tel/Fax: (Int. 064) (NZ 03) 332 4952
Tel: (Int. 64 3) (NZ 03) 738 0077

Women only. One double, one twin, one single bedrooms and one loft accommodation offering shared sleeping space. Dinner available. All special diets catered for. No smoking in house. Lodge B&B rates: $85.00 double, $50.00 single. Dinner $15.00 per person. Brochure and trip details available.

Roz and Cynthia run a women's outdoor adventure business, called Bushwise Women, from their bed and breakfast retreat, Bushline Lodge, set in 16 acres of land on the West Coast of the South Island. The Lodge is welcoming and has a unique kind of comfort and simplicity which nurture the body and nourish the spirit.

For guests who wish to simply enjoy the lodge and the surrounding area, there is angling, bushwalking, birdwatching, blowholes, blackwater and cave rafting, beachcombing, canoeing, cycling, caves, horsetrekking, kiwi house, potteries, swimming and the internationally acclaimed, TranzAlpine Railway.

Using the lodge as a base, guests can enjoy day trips of walks through the wonderful national parks close to the lodge. Based away from the lodge, there are sea kayaking, cross country skiing, tramping and bushwalking or bicycling trips. The women also run one Pacific Island holiday each year (eg 1997 - kayaking in Fiji).

Roz and Cynthia are trained in risk management, bushcraft, first aid and group work. Their combined 25 years of experience in a wide variety of outside pursuits ensures participants will feel safe and secure on all the adventures and trips on offer. The women's expertise extends to the kitchen where, after the day's activities, they prepare exquisite meals for the group. Cuisine is varied and emphasises gourmet vegetarian fare. Whether you are a couple seeking time alone together around the lodge in sympathetic surroundings, a group of friends needing a base for outdoor adventures, or a single woman looking for a bed and warm hearth, Bushline Lodge is an ideal retreat.

Richmond Hill House
22 Richmond Hill Road
Christchurch 8, New Zealand
Tel: 64 (03) 326 6862
Fax: 64 (03) 326 6432

**Women only holiday house. Two double, one single bedrooms.
TV. One shared bathroom. Sitting room. Washing machine,
telephone and iron. Smoking on decks or outside only. Tea and
coffee always available. No children. No pets. Other meals
available by arrangement. Special diets catered for with
advance notice. Open all year. B&B rates (including airport
transfers): $60.00 per night double occupancy. $40.00 for single
occupancy. Discounts for longer stays. Brochure available.**

Richmond Hill House is situated on the lower slopes of the hills in
the seaside village of Sumner, Christchurch. The hills form part of
Banks Peninsula, a wonderful area for walking, swimming, sailing
and relaxing. The house is quiet and private and comfortably
furnished and has all the facilities needed for total relaxation,
including a wonderful library, CD collection, TV and sun drenched
decks, all with views of the sea. It is ideally situated just three
minutes from the beach.

The village of Sumner looks out over Pegasus Bay and the blue
waters of the Pacific Ocean. The water is warm enough for
swimming in summer. The village has a small shopping centre,
cinema, coffee bars and restaurants and is twenty minutes from
Christchurch city centre.

Renowned for its 'English quality' Victorian Gothic buildings at the
heart of the city and the wonderful gardens found everywhere,
Christchurch is known as the Garden City of New Zealand. There
are many activities to enjoy locally, including an introduction to
Maori culture on the marae, walking the many bays and hills of
Banks Peninsula and observing whales, seals and penguins.

Your host, a teacher with an interest in music, the visual arts, travel
and trekking, specialises in warm, friendly, helpful hospitality. She
will be glad to pass on information about local lesbian groups, social
clubs, the arts, church groups and general local activities.

The Cottage
748 Portobello Road
Broad Bay, Dunedin
New Zealand
Tel: (03) 478 0073
Mobile 025 381 291

Women only B&B   Also, self-contained cottage with one double bedroom and en suite bathroom. Sitting room. No TV. Fully equipped kitchen. Garden. Telephone and iron. Hairdryer available. Dinner by arrangement. Special diets catered for with advance notice. No children. No pets. No smoking. Open throughout the year. Rates: B&B Double room is $85.00 per night.   Cottage also available to rent 'unserviced' at $60.00 per night or $360.00 per week.   Brochure available.

The two women run a B&B offering a double bedroom. Also available is The Cottage, which was originally built as a fisherman's retreat in the early 1900's. It is situated right on the harbour and offers private accommodation that is cosy and full of character.

There are an amazing number and variety of 'collectibles' in the cottage, many of which reflect the nostalgia of years gone by, including fascinating old tins and bottles in the kitchen and even the Edwardian travel wash kit in the bedroom. At the same time, the modern convenience of oodles of hot water, luxurious thick towels, a comfortable bed with fresh linen and electric blanket ensure a comfortable stay. The cottage's garden is perfectly balanced in texture, form and colour. It maintains the cottage's privacy but also allows beautiful vignettes of the harbour from the verandah.

There is a wonderful selection of books and games in the cottage for guests to enjoy during leisurely evenings, as well as a guitar for those who want to practice their chords!

Generous hamper breakfasts (included in the B&B price) are a speciality at the Cottage and prompt complimentary comments from guests. The breakfast can best be enjoyed on the verandah of this romantic cottage, overlooking the harbour and relax to the sound of waves lapping on the shore.

continued overleaf ...

The Cottage continued

Evening meals, may be self-catered, or provided by arrangement, or taken at one of the fine peninsula restaurants, many of which have a courtesy coach service.

Free range eggs and a variety of home grown produce is used in the preparation of meals and home made food is plentiful, including preserves, yoghurt and muesli. Coffee and teas are available for guests' use in the kitchen, as are herbs and spices for use in tea or cooking.

The cottage is at Broad Bay on the Otago Peninsula of the South Island. It is famous for its wildlife and the only mainland Royal Albatross colony in the world. Many New Zealand fur seals can be found here, including the world's rarest sea lion and the world's rarest penguin as well as the yellow eyed penguin and little blue penguins. Also nearby is New Zealand's only castle, Larnach Castle.

Visitors will have many walking tracks to enjoy, horseriding and empty, wild beaches to explore. Your hosts also have mountain bikes and kayaks available for hire. There are many opportunities to experience the area's nature and wildlife by joining various tours and cruises operated by local, women-run businesses. Qualified and well-informed women guides ensure that visitors are taken to areas of exceptional interest and beauty to enjoy all that the surroundings have to offer, including wonderful cliff formations, panoramic views, native plants and wildlife.

The two women owners are both English and have travelled extensively, finally choosing to settle in Broad Bay in 1988. They are interested in natural history, the environment, outdoor activities, art and collecting old world treasures. The cottage reflects the interests of the two women owners and will delight guests.

YOUR COMMENTS about your experience of an entry in Travel Her Way ~ Around the World.

We welcome your comments about any of the entries you have experienced in the book. Comments are used to provide positive or constructive feedback to the owners and organisers. We respect your right to anonymity and feedback is given in a general way - comments are not attributed to specific individuals.

I wish to comment about my/our experience of an entry in Travel Her Way ~ Around the World.

Entry name and page no. ....

Comments ....

....

....

....

....

....

Your name and telephone no. ....

Send to Travel Her Way,
17 Knotts Close, Dunstable, Beds, LU6 3NY

This page may be photocopied and forwarded to the above address

APPLYING FOR INCLUSION in the next edition of Travel Her Way ~ Around the World

To apply for an entry in our book you must be committed to supporting women travellers travelling alone, as couples and in groups. Your accommodation is preferably women only, women owned or women run. At the very least, women visitors to your establishment should feel welcomed, comfortable and safe.

For the benefit of our readers, premises will be visited by the authors or a designated female couple. The authors reserve the right to add a 'comment' to entries or to exclude entries. Submitting an application does not guarantee inclusion.

I wish to apply for inclusion in Travel Her Way ~ Around the World. I enclose a <u>stamped, self-addressed envelope</u> so that I can be sent a questionnaire and other information.

Name ....

Address ....

....

....

Telephone No. ....

**Send to Travel Her Way,
17 Knotts Close, Dunstable, Beds, LU6 3NY**

This page may be photocopied and forwarded to the above address